ASTROLOGY

ASTROLOGY
The Celestial Mirror

WARREN KENTON

THAMES AND HUDSON · LONDON

ART AND IMAGINATION
General Editor: Jill Purce

Printed in the Netherlands

ISBN 0 500 81004 4

Contents

For Judy

ACKNOWLEDGMENTS

Objects in the plates are reproduced by courtesy of the following:
Bibliothèque Nationale 20
British Museum 5, 6, 10, 14, 16, 25, 39, 48, 55, 57, 58, 61
Biblioteca Apostolica Vaticana 15
Biblioteca Estense, Modena 27, 28, 29, 30, 31, 32, 33
Hessisches Museum, Kassel 50
Huntington Library, San Marino 34
Louvre 3
Metropolitan Museum, New York 2
Museo Archeologico, Florence 11
Musée Condé, Chantilly 36, 42, 43
Musée de l'Evêché, Bayeux 23
Musée National du Bardo, Tunisia 12
Musée du Vieil Orbe, Orbe, Switzerland 7
Museum of the History of Science, Oxford 51, 52, 53
Palazzo Schifanoia, Ferrara 35
Pinacoteca Vaticana 59
Science Museum, London 60
Selçuk Museum, Turkey 8
Staatliche Museen, Berlin (East) 19
Trinity College Library, Dublin 18
Victoria and Albert Museum 54

Photographs are by the following:
Alinari 11; figs. 45, 46, 47, 50
Department of the Environment, Crown Copyright 4; fig. 66
Giraudon 3, 23, 26, 36, 42, 43, 46; figs. 38, 39
Sonia Halliday 8, 12
André Held 7
Hirmer Fotoarchiv fig. 2
Huntington Library of San Marino 34
Mansell Collection figs. 5, 7, 19
Orlandini 27, 28, 29, 30, 31, 32, 33
NASA 62
John Reader 1
Scala 24, 35, 47
Staatsbibliothek, Berlin 45
Eileen Tweedy 51, 52, 53
Warburg Institute fig. 57

The Celestial Mirror

1 Beginnings

From the earliest times the sky has intrigued man, even the most primitive hunter pausing to contemplate the all-enclosing canopy of the heavens. To the prehistoric thinker the sky probably appeared to be the highest ruler. Day and night issued from it, as did the seasonal round. Nature was subject to its governance; from horizon to horizon everything on earth was sealed in by a celestial cave-roof that continually filled and emptied of a myriad strange and fearsome entities composed of fire, wind and water. The sky was always there above, omnipotent.

By the time men lived in tribal communities, sky-watching was part of life; the seasonal changes marked by the longest and shortest days (the solstices), and by the times when night and day were equal in length (the equinoxes), became a simple calendar for hunting and planting. Besides these useful routine cycles, the position or state of the sun or moon was noted at the time of significant events, and these observations were handed down to become part of tribal history. As the body of knowledge increased it was seen that certain phenomena in the heavens coincided with particular happenings on earth, so that these parallels became fused into signs of omen. Total eclipses or blood-red moons became associated with bad harvests or massacres, and no chief could afford to disregard such warnings.

Everywhere on earth fables arose populating the skies with gods, demons and heroes. Gradually the heavens were hung with myths, every people adding its own version, until eventually in each culture a complex hierarchy of celestial beings was formulated, who watched, judged and manipulated the lives of men below.

When men began to live consistently in one place, temples were built to honour these gods. Name days, which we retain to the present, were given to the chief among them, and festivals were celebrated to placate the apparently moody deities who could send famine, wars and pestilence as well as good harvests and peace. Sometimes the festivals were carefully timed sacrifices to aid, for instance, the sun in his unending conflict with his dark foe at the winter solstice. It was hoped he would repay his human allies, who were dependent on his good will, with bountiful crops.

As civilization progressed, the priests who kept the calendars continually perfected their celestial records. This required the methodical study of the sky. Connecting the stars near to each other into constellations was probably at first a visually convenient grouping. These, according to each culture, became figured into images familiar to local mythology. The constellations were also used as the background markers to the movement of the sun, the moon and the five odd stars that wandered to and fro among their static fellows. It was realized that the sun progressed through the stars along a band of particular constellations, as did the moon and the five other wandering stars (or planets). This band, which we know as the zodiac, was traversed once a year by the sun and once a month by the moon. It appeared to circle not only the heavens but the earth also. Any given constellation in the zodiac was seen at night only at certain times of the year. It followed that in summer the sun must be in the region of the constellations visible in winter, and vice versa. Such a conclusion gave a logic to an overall picture of the heavens that was slowly crystallizing out of centuries of record-keeping.

The Babylonians divided the zodiac into eighteen sections, other cultures into more or less in number. Eventually it was fixed at twelve, a compromise between the thirteen annual cycles of the moon and the single passage of the sun. From this arose the zodiac as we know it, the sun spending around thirty days in each constellation. It was further subdivided into 360 degrees, the sun moving a degree a day with four or five days to spare. These days out of time were easily absorbed by the solstice and equinox and other festivals. Our chronological and dating systems originate from this period.

2 The Gods

Astrology and astronomy in early times were one. While the celestial movements were measured, corresponding natural cycles were discerned to have inherent principles. The rapid growth of spring was matched by decay in the autumn; and the seed in the rotting fruit contained the life for the next year's cycle. Such observations were directly related to the position of the sun, and gradually the symbols that composed the constellations began to change from purely mythological motifs into glyphs that described the character of that particular time of year.

As far back as nomadic times it had been noted that the planets which moved like courtiers round the sun and moon made erratic motions, sometimes passing each other at great speed, at others slowing down and even going backwards. Because of this, early observers naturally paid them great attention, gradually building up not only a picture of their rhythms among the constellations, but a case record of their position, brightness and angle in relation to earthly events. In time they were given the status of gods, with archetypal symbols to describe their performance.

The symbol in ancient times was what modern technological language is to us. It was the synthesis, in word or image, of the principles underlying a body of knowledge. This is borne out in our subject by the fact that in many unconnected places the same ideas were associated with each planet and its planetary god. Thus the Babylonian goddess Nana is quite recognizable in the Astarte of the Phoenicians, the Ishtar of the Assyrians and the Aphrodite of the Greeks. All these archetypes, or associations of ideas, relate to the planet Venus, which with its beauty and fluctuation is seen as female and young. This may seem a superficial connection; but the law of archetypes, that of the psychological response to an identical universal principle, embodied Venus in a similar image all over the world.

To give some idea how a symbol was generated, a visual appreciation of each planet is useful. Mercury's tiny point of light moves in a rapid, tight loop, the loop motion against Venus's more brilliant but slower see-sawing, six-monthly rhythm. Mars, the red ember of a planet with his two-year cycle, periodically flares up in magnitude as he abruptly approaches and retreats from the earth. Jupiter, on the other hand, moves his huge bright presence in measured tread along the zodiac, while Saturn, the outermost of the visible planets, is the slowest of the wanderers, his distant lantern dull in comparison as he plods his thirty-year journey round the heavens. These characteristics gave rise to the complex set of archetypes known as the planetary gods, whose cosmic principles work both above and below: in the heavens and in the world of man.

Mercury, whom the Greeks called Hermes, was the personification of nimble mind, sharp wit, communication and speech. Seen in the image of a restless youth who picked up, then dropped, whatever came his way, he was considered the principle behind the senses. As messenger of the gods, he informed them about happenings in the world and conveyed their response. In continuous motion, he was for ever collecting, remembering and forgetting as he passed through endless shallow love affairs. This describes symbolically the mercurial part of man. Close to the sun, he was chameleon-like, taking on whatever interested him at that moment. God of curiosity, he carried the caduceus, a rod denoting all the skills of information, from magic to statistics. He was given the rulership over travel, trade, communication, general knowledge, virtuosity and sharp practice. Equally patron of thieves and businessmen, he quickly took on the ethics of those about him, be they planets or people. Concerned less with consequences than present excitement, he was a bright messenger of cunning and irresponsibility.

The archetypal image for Venus was that of a powerful, naked young woman. One of the goddesses behind nature, her principle was the power of instinct, attraction and repulsion, as expressed in the endless round of the seasons. In spring and summer she put on leaves and flowers, and she laid them aside in the autumn and winter. She drew beasts together to fight and mate in momentary passion. Among men she was the goddess not so much of love as of sensuality and pleasure. Young men and maidens prayed to her. As Mercury was the god of childhood, so Venus was the deity of youth, with all its passionate desires and hates. Good food, comfort and pleasure were her *métier*; deprivation and ugliness she abhorred. Her gifts to those who could control the venerean part of themselves were the powers of beauty, art and harmony. On Olympus she was regarded with caution. Wife of the ugly Vulcan, she brought trouble with her need for pleasure. When bored she was violent, indolent and self-indulgent, exhibiting the characteristics that appear in gifted but temperamental creators and in courtesans. Considered in astrology as the 'lesser benefic', she was a mixed blessing.

Mars is usually cast in the role of god of war. Although true, this can be misleading, for Venus often precipitates a fight that Mars, the disciplined warrior, has to finish. To be as passionate as he is often made to appear would not make a good soldier. Small in stature, he was originally depicted as a powerful dark being with sword and shield ready for action. Here we must learn to read the meaning of the symbol. Power, smallness and dark colouring indicate dynamism in a controlled, passive state, like a coiled spring. The shield is to resist and the sword to protect. Defence is a soldier's only real justification for existence. Mars's failure in war against the goddess of wisdom indicates that on that occasion he mistook his role. Regarded in astrology as the 'lesser malefic', he has, like all the other planets, a positive and a negative side. In man he is concerned with judgment and discipline. His gift is courage, but only for a just cause. A badly positioned Mars in a horoscope indicates too much or too little control. The Romans adopted Mars as their patron, and the rise and fall of their empire well illustrates the working of the martial principle. When Rome ceased to maintain its laws, corruption set in, followed by cruelty and all the negative qualities of Mars. His period for an individual was manhood.

Jupiter, the largest and most majestic of the planets, was the Egyptian god Ammon and the Zeus of the Greeks. His powerful light and his legendary magnificence made him the king of the gods and the 'greater benefic' of men. This generous image included flaws, in that his largesse could be destructive. He once blasted a mistress out of existence with too much glory. Usually depicted as a figure of mature power, Jupiter occasionally threw thunderbolts that did not always hit their target. So that, although he was a beneficent influence, it was not always advisable to attract his attention. Here again are the positive and negative aspects of a god. Moreover, while acknowledged as the lord of Olympus, Jupiter could not control his wife. This myth suggests that even his majesty was not all-powerful, a crucial concept when all the planetary gods are seen in relation to one another. Here is the idea that no god may dominate, although he or she may have their day of moment. In astrology Jupiter was considered an important factor in aiding men and nations to become great. His power gave men good heart, the desire for wealth and empire. Jupiter at his best was magnanimity and expansion, and at his worst indulgence and over-dispersal. In men he represents deep emotion, mercy and charity. His period was middle age.

Saturn or Chronos was the god of time. His slow movement gave him the image of an old man. He personified age, rigidity and gravity. This gave him the role of 'greater malefic' in astrology. To the wise he was the god of understanding and experience, his scythe of death not just the harvesting of generations but also the clearing away of the old and useless. Being the least erratic of the celestial bodies, he was credited with constancy and long sight, for as oldest god he had seen all the cycles many times. Originally the king of the solar system, he had been banished by Jupiter to the outer court where he drags his rings round the heavens. To some he was a dismal god, to others the great teacher. His schooling was hard but just. Old age, the period associated with Saturn, could be a time of reflection rather than misery. A mentor over nations and individuals, his influence was seen in periods of restriction. On the positive side he was considered to be the preserver of customs that held a community together during grim times. Endurance and hard work were his virtues, and as such he was regarded as the patron of the Jews, who possess all the saturnine qualities of labour, respect of law, forbearance in suffering and love of tradition. As the god of time, a well-positioned Saturn in a horoscope guaranteed long life. In psychological terms he was the reflective intellect. For this reason he was sometimes called the Watcher on the Threshold.

The sun and moon were considered differently from the planets. Divinities of light, they had dominion in the realms of day and night, their relationship echoing that of male and female in the natural world and the cosmic active and passive principles in the supernatural. Sometimes seen in conflict, at others in complement, the pattern of their heavenly marriage was of great importance to mankind, and around them a wide and ancient mythology created an elaborate pair of archetypes.

The sun, brilliant deity of the day, had many images. To some he was the fiery eye of God; to others a flaming chariot or a winged sphere of incandescence. By Greek times his many names and forms had been resolved into the archetype of Apollo, the golden young man whose blinding glance none but the honest could meet. Sometimes carrying a lyre and bow, he was the symbol of light and truth, his divine insight penetrating the darkest corners of world and man. Beautiful but terrible in aspect, Apollo represented man's heart of hearts, that shining centre of the inner human solar system. Here was a man's spiritual sun. This is why, in astrology, the position of the sun is of prime importance. Of all the gods, Apollo was perhaps – like a man's relationship to himself – the least understood. This is because most people cannot face the Apollo in themselves, cannot bear the truth about their lives. Such observation required integrity and the high courage to live out one's fate. Most prefer to live with the illusions of the moon, the pale reflection of the real thing. Apollo was the god of divination, the blinding moment of truth that can change the direction of a life. As the sun god he ripened the fruits and corn, but when afflicted he could burn; this same capability could heal. Pride was his chief fault, for although he was the god of prophecy, truth may sometimes be used incorrectly. As a master of the lyre Apollo played divine music, and this we perceive every day in the emanations of the sun. His age was a man's prime.

The moon had many mythological aspects. In most societies she took the role of consort to the sun, though it was accepted that her rule was as powerful in its passive way. Her influence, it was believed, operated principally at night and in a monthly sequence, her waxing and waning evoking a daily and monthly pulse of growth in plants and in the movement of animals. Over men she held the wand of dreams, magic, madness and love. Over women she had special rule, working through their menstrual cycle. Goddess of birth and death, she was considered a receptor rather than an initiator, her fast motion acting as a counterbalance, a pendulum of ebb and flow that moved the seas and nature in a gentle but powerful rhythm. In the inner solar system of psychological archetypes in man, the moon principle was the reflection by which we see ourselves and the outer world. Here is the ego, the ordinary mind, as against the inner self of the sun of our natures. Goddess of sex and imagination, Luna, Diana, Selene and Artemis, the many aspects of the moon principle govern most people's lives as they live out a rhythmic pattern of cyclic drives and illusions. Mythology tells how the moon fell in love with Endymion or mankind, the shepherd of nature. But she could not possess him except when he was asleep. Therefore she set out to enchant him and so enjoy his company in day as well as night dreams. As Hecate, goddess of witchcraft, she has the power to hold most people in the prison of ego with its illusions about itself. Because of this the moon pulls not only the seas but the masses of mankind into tides of work and play, peace and war, and all the mechanical rhythms that bind men into the plant and animal level of existence. When Diana was once observed by the mortal Actaeon in her nakedness she set the hounds upon him. No enchantress cares to be exposed. For this reason the goddess of the moon was loved and feared. The moon ruled the age of babyhood.

3 Cosmology

About 3000 BC the Sumerian civilization formalized its idea of the universe into a total world-picture. In it the earth was surrounded by water, with the stars, planets, sun and moon hovering in a domecapped firmament. Mankind was ruled by the gods in heaven above, through the celestial bodies and elements. This model was the working hypothesis for early astrology. When the rational Greeks inherited this cosmology, it underwent various modifications. Thus, Thales, born around 640 BC, constructed a model without any reference to the gods, while Anaximander produced a cosmology of fire enclosed by mist with a solid cold mass at its centre. Working half-way between Western intellect and Eastern imagination, Pythagoras saw the universe as consciousness and energy slowly descending into matter. The planets and stars, he said, were living intelligences, their bodies, like men's, the vehicles of a spiritual being. He went on to say that the planets made music. Such a concept was quite natural to a school of thought that saw everything as a harmonious expression of one godhead. Even the elements had their perfect geometry; the tetrahedron for fire, the octahedron for air, the icosahedron for water and the cube for earth. As for man, the Pythagoreans saw him as a miniature version of Creation, resonating to the tones emitted by the planets above. This macro-microcosmic view perhaps came from the Judaic Bible, which said that man was made in God's image. The cross-connection could have been made by Pythagoras during his travels in the Middle East.

In Greece astrology, imported from the Orient, had considerable effect on philosophy. Heraclitus, a disciple of Aristotle, wrote on the sun as the source of vital forces; Plato considered the sun and moon in relation to the sexes; and Hippocrates maintained that no doctor was qualified if he could not interpret a patient's horoscope.

By the time of the astronomer Ptolemy, in the second century AD, the various world models had crystallized into a geocentric hybrid based on the perfect shape of sphere and number. In this scheme, which came to be called the Ptolemaic world view, the earth was surrounded by the elements of water, air and fire. Above this was the crystalline sphere of the moon, which circled below those of the sun and the five planets. Enclosing this cosmic onion were the sphere of fixed stars and the sphere of the 'Prime Mover' which enveloped the total scheme. Beyond was heaven, the home of the gods. This concept of the universe was accepted for more than a thousand years.

When the Greeks improved on the measurements of the Oriental astronomer-astrologers, discrepancies were found. Hipparchus discovered when dividing the zodiac into its twelve 30-degree sections that certain stars had shifted two degrees in 150 years in relation to the first degree of Aries. This was important because it meant there were two zodiacs, one orientated to the sun, the other to the constellations. In time there could be no real correspondence between the astrologers' moving 'tropical zodiac', which reflects the sun's position in relation to the earth, and the fixed stellar constellations.

The zodiac, Greek for 'circle of animals', by this time had been slowly evolved by observation into twelve symbols that expressed the terrestrial situation when the sun was in that part of the sky. Thus the sign of Aries, the Ram, shows in its sudden rush the initial appearance of the spring corn, while Taurus, the Bull, defines the gathering charge and growth of plants and mating of animals. Gemini, the Twins, describe the proliferation and interconnection of the ecological pyramid. With the sun in Cancer, the Crab, nature is full of liquid succulence, each plant and animal charged with the sap of life. At high summer Leo the Lion's strength and mane demonstrate the sun's fiery power. This is followed by the Virgin, symbol of the harvest and the seed for next year's season. The sign of Libra, the Scales, marks the autumnal equinox, as summer's heat becomes milder before the cooling decay of nature turns into the sign of death in Scorpio. Sagittarius carries the year on to a period of reflection, indicated by the archer looking back as he gallops towards the winter solstice. The fish-goat sign of Capricorn denotes the transition point from the old to the new as the sun begins to climb again. The man pouring water on to the ground, Aquarius, is the time of the winter rains, and the Fishes, Pisces, indicate the living but unseen movements beneath the soaking earth which precede Aries and the first day of spring, the beginning of the cycle.

The connection between the seasons and people born at certain times had been noted and developed by Ptolemy's period, far beyond such basic initial observations as that winter children tended to be more reserved and tougher than those born in summer. Careful documentation slowly built up a pattern that synthesized into twelve broad types roughly corresponding to each sign of the zodiac, but in terms of temperament. This system however was complicated by factors other than the sun position. True, each man had a recognizable type, but people born even on the same day were not identical. This indicated that the moon and the planets as well as the sun might affect a person's psyche. It took many centuries of objective correlation to arrive at a system which took all influences into account. While some astrologers studied effects – appearances and phenomena – others worked from causes or first principles. The latter argued that as man was a little world he must, according to the esoteric maxim 'as above so below', contain and respond to the great world that contained him. Therefore it followed that the positions of the sun, moon and planets at the moment of birth – or of conception – must form a distinct crystallization of the psyche as it emerged into the world of matter. The issue between conception and birth was eventually decided by the time factor. No one could know exactly when a child was conceived; and so most astrologers took the first breath as the moment to observe the sky, and based their empirical observations on data collected in this way. From this the earliest true horoscopes were drawn up.

I shall take one sign as an example. The sun in Scorpio in the northern hemisphere catches the last of autumn. Everywhere trees and plants shed their dying leaves. There is a smell of decay everywhere, and yet there are seeds in the rotting husks and fruits; life is waiting to regenerate. In a man born at this time there is the same set of principles. The Scorpio has both the destructive and regenerative in his nature. He has a powerful sex drive and is fascinated by death. Zealous against corruption, he will cut open everything, even himself, to find new possibilities. He is a warrior and surgeon, a killer and healer, an ender and beginner of life. These attributes are only a fraction of those observed in a pure scorpionic type, which like all pure types is very rare.

The twelve signs of the zodiac recur repeatedly in ancient literature, although they are not always obvious. It is said that the twelve tribes of Israel and the twelve disciples describe, again in symbolic language, the full zodiacal circle of humanity. The idea was carried over into the jury system, so that a man was tried by a balanced assessment of every type of man. Alas, the original concept has been lost.

The Jews, always a speculative people, made an indirect contribution to astrology despite their ban on its practice. Ezekiel's vision (Ezekiel, 1) was interpreted by Kabbalists as a view of four worlds, or levels, which compose the universe. These worlds interpenetrated, so that the *Book of Formation*, written about the time of Ptolemy, spoke in biblical and astrological terms of the connections and reciprocal influences which affect everything in the universe. This conception gave philosophical validity to astrological metaphysics, by then a complete contrast to the degenerate and superstitious astrology being practised in the market-place.

The four elements of earth, water, air and fire were seen by the Greeks as mixed states of materiality, always seeking equilibrium, which interacted in man and throughout nature. This led astrologers to the idea that each sign was sympathetic to a particular element. In time, sets or triads of elemental sympathies were incorporated into astrology, each element being identified with three of the twelve zodiacal signs. Thus Capricorn had an affinity through earth with Taurus and Virgo, while Pisces, Cancer and Scorpio interacted through water. Air was the link between Aquarius, Gemini and Libra, and fire between Aries, Leo and Sagittarius. Out of this another set of relationships emerged. Here the elements and their signs paired in opposites, so that earthy Capricorn complemented watery Cancer, airy Aquarius matched its zodiac opposite, the fiery Leo, and so on round the circle. This created yet another sub-system, linking the signs in fours to form three crosses, which became known as the fixed, mutable and cardinal crosses. These three definitions were related to the ancient idea of an active, a passive and a connecting principle behind the workings of the universe. From the astrological view the cardinal signs were active, the fixed passive and the mutables the connectors. Thus the cardinal Capricorn or Aries would initiate an enterprise, the fixed Taurus or Leo hold it on course, and the mutable Pisces or Virgo make the conditions for change.

These interlocking sub-schemes added a qualitative depth to astrology: for example, the earthy signs were practical by nature, the watery emotional, the airy intellectual and the fiery inspirational. This corresponded to the four humours which governed traditional psychology: phlegmatic (earthy), melancholy (watery), sanguine (airy) and choleric (fiery).

Another major idea which crystallized in this period was that of the celestial sphere. Taking the Sumerian notion of a heavenly dome, astronomers projected up from the earth an imaginary globe with meridians, equator and tropics of Cancer and Capricorn engraved upon it. This enabled the motions of the heavens to be plotted in celestial longitudes and latitudes. It was a geocentric concept of the universe, but quite acceptable from man's view because it placed him at the centre. As the first theory of relativity, it put man, as the observer, at the focus of the upper world's influence, and this lent power to the arguments of astrology.

Celestial influences were the effects on earth of particular planets in certain signs. Thus Mars in Aries and Scorpio seemed to stimulate action in nations and in individuals; Jupiter, powerful in Pisces and Sagittarius, was weak in their opposites, Virgo and Gemini. Saturn was constructive in Capricorn but a very bad influence in Cancer. Out of a long process of observation came a table of effects which was graduated in terms of four categories: in exaltation, strong, in detriment, and in fall. Added to these effects were the geometric relationships between the planets. Great lovers of geometry and mathematics, the Greek astrologers detected that when planets were at particular angles to each other tensions and eases of tension occurred, rather like those between people when passing each other. These were identified with precise angles based on the 360° circle of the zodiac. The negative or inauspicious relationships appeared to be oppositions (180°) and squares (90°). Thus, Saturn in Aries, in opposition to Jupiter (in Libra) or square to Mars (in Capricorn), constituted a 'bad aspect'. Good aspects were trine (120°) and sextile (60°). These relationships, coupled with the status of each planet in sign, element, cross, enhancement and affliction, created a complex of factors which was summarized in a graphic form known as a horoscope. Obviously, much knowledge was required for its analysis. Here the skilled astrologers, or Chaldeans, as they were called, came in as professionals.

The date of the first real individual horoscope is unknown. However, certainly by Greek times it had reached its recognizable form. For erecting a chart it was necessary to make a picture of the sky at the time being considered (which, for an individual, was that of birth). To do this required the plotting of the position of the planets, sun and moon in the zodiac on that day. Further, their height above the horizon had to be considered, for it was noted that their strength was greater when they were close to the meridian, where a planet could be as powerful in its own way as the sun in mid-heaven. This led the horoscope to be divided into quadrants based on the meridian and horizon lines, with each quarter taking on a rising or declining character. It was also recognized that planets and signs on the eastern horizon had a particular power. This was called the ascendant. Out of this juxtaposition of celestial forces the astrologer had to interpret a clear picture of a situation or life. This was not easy, because there were still many unresolved arguments about the nature of man, who was subject not only to mineral, vegetable and animal laws within himself but to his own elemental humour. All these questions had no neat answer, especially since people could be educated in different ways or be subject to social and family pressures.

To the thoughtful astrologer individual fortunes were not the only issue: he concerned himself with man's purpose and position in the universe. While most astrologers continued to study phenomena, the philosophical tried to understand what generated them. Out of this came two kinds of serious astrology: those of the practical Aristotelian line, based on observation, and those sympathetic to the mystical Platonic approach. Ptolemy summed up the Aristotelian approach in his work the *Tetrabiblos*, which is a collection of examples and notes on nativities, diseases, marriages and deaths. Also included are articles on the signs of nations, on weather-forecasting and the prediction of future events, length of life and material fortune. As the synthesis of ancient astrological data, the work later became the scholarly basis of Arab and Western astrology. Of the esoteric approach to astrology we have little documentary evidence, as the knowledge was normally transmitted orally from master to initiated disciple. The Kabbalistic *Book of Formation* gives some hints of a cosmological system, but to a reader without the vital key, and without the level of spiritual development required, it remains meaningless. Here metaphysics gives way to direct experience, and astrology is seen as the interacting laws of a total unity.

4 *Ascendant*

With the break-up of the Roman empire, organized knowledge began to fragment. Into this vacuum came early Christianity, which had no use for pagan ideas, least of all astrology. Indeed, the new priesthood fought astrology on the grounds that its fatalism directly opposed the divine intervention of Christ. Astrological influence can, however, be seen in the Revelation of St John, notably in the images associated with the four Evangelists, which may well be Kabbalistic in origin. At the eastern end of the empire some pagan elements remained in the culture, and it was some time before the heavens were repeopled with angels and archangels. Astrology, declined, either by discouragement or persecution, until only Ptolemy's *Tetrabiblos* recorded the centuries of labour.

As Western Europe moved into its Dark Age, Islamic Arabia expanded in a conquest of war and religion. After initially destroying rival concepts, it discovered and adopted classical Greek learning. Among the works translated into Arabic was the *Tetrabiblos*, and the Arabs, realizing their astronomical ignorance, were inspired to begin a new period of celestial study.

While perfecting their lunar calendar, they improved astronomical tools, producing exquisite astrolabes of brass that could precisely fix the altitude of a star and so find the direction of Mecca. They became enamoured with astrology. Indeed, interest in the sky was so great that Arab rulers from Spain to Samarkand built observatories to improve Greek star maps. Many of the names of stars, such as Betelgeuse and Rigel, and terms like nadir and zenith, come from this period.

For some, astrological study became a necessity, despite their faith in Allah's will. Every Caliph wanted a glimpse into the book of fate, and astrologers arose to meet the need. These included men with new ideas, the most important of which was the system of mundane houses. This refines on Ptolemy's system of quadrants by subdividing the sky into twelve sections, six above the horizon and six below. This gave not only a more accurate picture of the positions of the sun, moon and planets at the place and hour under consideration, but a precise time plot of the zodiac itself as it rotated through a twenty-four-hour cycle. The scheme became a standard grid, every chart adopting the idea that, while all the celestial bodies varied in position, this set of divisions was constant for any given point on earth. Like the ascending and descending quadrants of Ptolemy, each of the twelve sectors or 'houses' had a particular effect on the signs and celestial bodies posited in it at a given moment. For instance, any planet near the meridian was powerful, but on each side in a different way. Moreover, any luminary or planet just above the ascendant (the eastern horizon) in a horoscope tended to make a person reserved, whereas if it were just below the reverse was the case. Further examination revealed that the characteristics of the twelve houses corresponded to those of the zodiac signs, but that they were arranged in reverse order. Thus, the astrological year begins with Aries in spring, goes on to Cancer at midsummer, Libra in autumn, and Capricorn at midwinter and ends in Pisces; but in its daily round the sun enters the twelfth house (that of the ascendant, corresponding to Pisces) at 6 a.m., leaves the tenth (wintry Capricorn) at high noon, descends from the seventh (Libra) to the sixth (Virgo) at 6 p.m., and passes from the fourth house (that of Cancer) to the third (Gemini) at midnight; the house of Aries (4–6 a.m.) is the last. (This is on a time-perfect day.)

This system was called that of the mundane houses because each house appertained directly to worldly matters, there being a distinction between the moving zodiac, which defined the psyche, and the fixed grid of the houses, which governed the manifestations of the psyche in the world. The sun might, for example, be in Leo the autocrat, but if it was also in the twelfth mundane house, that of privacy, the talent for leadership would be thwarted. A person born with the sun in Virgo tends towards modesty; but if the sun is in the tenth house he may achieve much by virtue of his very modesty. Each house was given an area of worldly domain. Thus, the first (Aries) was concerned with appearances; it is the threshold of the day. The second (Taurus) was concerned with growth and possessions, the third (Gemini) with communications, relatives and short journeys. The fourth house (Cancer) appertained to security and domestic matters, the fifth (Leo) to children, leadership and entertainment. The sixth house (Virgo) was that of health and work; Libra embodied the principle underlying the seventh house in matters of law and partnership. Scorpio, the eighth, was the sign of the house of death, and all matters appertaining to the invisible world; while the ninth house, that of Sagittarius, the most reflective sign in the zodiac, was related to religion, philosophy and distant travel, both physical and metaphysical. Capricorn, with its ambitious nature, gave rise to the tenth house, that of achievement, through which the sun passes at noon. The eleventh house was associated with Aquarius, the sign of sociability and fellowship. The twelfth house of Pisces was perceived as relating to privacy, secrets and hidden things.

From these refinements came the explanation why the sun sign expressed itself differently even in people born on the same day in the same year, but at different hours and places. It also showed why a man could be well favoured in particular fields despite the bad positions of sun and moon, and how, because of his ascendant, a man might appear what he was not. The ascendant, it seemed, was a kind of body type, and even more a mask than the personality created by the ego (the moon) which overlay the sun of a man's essential being. Any planet on the ascendant was a major consideration, as was the sign in the first house at the time of birth. If Mars or Scorpio were there, for example, the appearance would be smallish, the brow dark and the eyes sharp. Moreover, if Mars were afflicted (i.e. in an unfavourable sign, house or aspect), the whole demeanour could be negative and aggressive.

Other examples of the mundane house system at work show the secondary action of the planets. Saturn in the second house (that of possessions) spells financial hardship. This applies in general, but most particularly to the person *born* with Saturn in this position, for whom it recurs at the ages of twenty-nine and sixty. Jupiter in the second house is highly auspicious, especially if the zodiac sign in the house is sympathetic to the planet. If an earth sign is in the second house, the possessions involved are practical; if water, they are emotional attachments; if air, they are ideas; if fire, they are the talents possessed to inspire.

In the seventh house Saturn's presence would delay partnerships, but if well placed in relation to other bodies it could mature relationships in business as well as in marriage. Here again, the element corresponding to the sign plays a part in determining the nature of the influence.

According to the mundane house system no people except those born within four minutes of each other in the same place could lay claim to the same fate. Even in twins this occurrence is rare. With the ascendant moving a degree every four minutes, several planets may have risen or set, and in an hour three or four signs can cross the mid-heaven. The mundane house system gives a precise image of the sky at that moment in that place. No one else can occupy that unique time-space-equation, except in rare cases, which, when followed through, have proved the rule: the individuals have shared their fates despite social differences.

While the mundane system was being worked out disagreement arose, not over the principle so much as over how to divide up the sectors: astrologers differed on the geometric formulae. This confusion brought dissension into the profession and created a bad image; the problem still exists today.

As techniques improved, directional or predictive astrology generated opposition; to give information about a man's fate might do more harm than good. For example, if one predicted that a man would enter a marital crisis at forty, it might stop him correcting the condition. Likewise, a man expecting good fortune in a particular year might become lazy. Besides, it was argued, it was God's prerogative to determine the future. This was countered by the injunction 'know thyself'; for astrology is a key to one's nature. Prognostication must not be carried too far; but a man can use the knowledge to study himself through the expression of his life. In this way, said some astrologers, he could become master of his fate. Acceptance of God's will is in no way incompatible with knowing who one is and what is required of one in the world, as indicated by the natal chart. Needless to say, there have always been the gullible, who daily visit their astrologers; but the wise say that a man should follow his inner sun.

5 Morning

As Islam developed its high civilization, Christendom passed through a dark period. Even in the Eastern Church, where ancient Greek texts still existed, they were neglected in consequence of the Church's anti-paganism. The Church's ban, of course, included astrology. As the year of the millennium approached there was great expectation of the Second Coming of Christ. But it passed uneventfully, leaving the strength of pure faith weakened. Halley's Comet came and went in 1066, and nothing happened except the conquest of England. The Church was in a restless condition. Faith was not enough: knowledge was required, and this could be obtained from the Arabs. In Spain many cities had universities where subjects ranging from mathematics to theology were studied. Here also Sufis, the mystics of Islam, shared Greek ideas with the Jewish Kabbalists; and those Christians who were capable of seeing beyond the sectarian view visited Toledo and Cordova and other cities where real knowledge was being discussed. With the Crusades, and new contacts between the split churches of Rome and Byzantium, knowledge also began to flow in from the East. The Western Church was placed in a dilemma. Revelation had been sufficient up to then, but now it could not ignore reason; it had to find a solution that met the needs of the intellect and strengthened the heart.

In the mid thirteenth century St Thomas Aquinas formulated a synthesis that combined Aristotelian logic with Christian mystery. This solution, influenced by the Kabbalah and by Sufic thought, saw Creation as a great ladder stretching between heaven and earth. The upper end was composed of angelic beings who governed the lower worlds of stars, sun, planets and moon, which in turn ruled the sub-inner spheres of elements, animals, plants and stones. All creation was an integrated chain of living, with each level serving a divine plan, and at the centre was man, the image of God. This hierarchical view was acceptable to the Church because it reflected the spiritual and temporal organization of feudal society.

The scholastic philosophy of Aquinas thus Christianized the Ptolemaic cosmology. The mineral, plant and animal levels were linked with various states of man on the carnal plane of existence. The soul was a reflection of the upper world: this meant that it was affected by the realms above the moon, including the zodiac itself. Man was again seen as a microcosm, with the various signs of the zodiac assigned to parts of the body. Thus Aries as the beginning of the year was the head, while Taurus related to the neck and shoulders. Gemini, the dual air sign, ruled the arms and lungs, and the watery

Cancer ruled the breast and stomach. Leo governed the hot, solar heart of the body, while Virgo, the earthy sign of practical work, governed the abdomen. The sign of Libra, the Scales, related symbolically to the hips, just as the stinging action of Scorpio referred to the sex organs. Sagittarius, the galloping archer, was assigned to the thighs; the earthy Capricorn was seen in the bony structure of the body (as manifest in the knees). Aquarius corresponded to the shins, the upright posture of man; and the two fishes of Pisces matched the shape of the feet. This astrological model, despite its pagan origin, served to confirm the doctrine that 'God created Adam in his own image'.

With scholasticism astrology became popular. Indeed, professorships were created in the new universities, and the great French scholar Abelard went so far as to give his love-child by Heloise the name of Astrolabe. By the fifteenth century astrology had become deeply established in medieval life, and the Church borrowed many astrological motifs. Its festivals had, after all, always followed an astronomical cycle, with Easter as the spring resurrection and Christmas the festival of the winter solstice. Churches were naturally laid on an east-west axis, a temple tradition older than the Christian idea of facing in the direction of Jerusalem.

In secular life the idea of fate fascinated everyone, for there were none who were not directly affected by the seasons, or aware of rhythms either in crops, trade or the fortunes of nations. Those who could afford it employed astrologers, and those who could not bought calendars or almanacs from fairground charlatans. Such consultations were not without cause in a time when plagues and wars frequently wiped out whole communities. Fatalism was widespread: the Black Death reduced the population of England by half, and the Church took the view that it was a divine punishment. All men were subject to the wheel of fortune, some gaining, some losing, a few receiving the momentary crown of success at the zenith of the wheel before it plunged down. This recurring symbol of a wheel often included the seven gods, each deity having his period of influence in the cycle of ascendancy and decline. The ancient idea of celestial rulers was quite acceptable to medieval society, which saw all things ranked in their proper place. In such a hierarchical scheme it was natural that the angels should work through the celestial realm which oversaw the world below. Indeed, not only did each man have his dominant humour and his astrological sign, but even his profession was governed by a planet. The miners had Saturn as their patron, and surgeons and soldiers had Mars. Venus had a particular rule over artists and musicians, while Jupiter related to clerics and kings. Even thieves had their planet in Mercury, sharing the same planetary god as shopkeepers and printers.

On a greater scale, just as Ptolemy had ascribed zodiacal signs to various peoples, so the same celestial patronage was applied to old and new cities. Aquinas said that angels watched over men and great enterprises, so it seemed reasonable that cities should be accorded the same privilege. In many cases the dates of founding had been noted, so strong is man's sense of beginning things; and from these dates many cities identified their zodiac signs. Under Aries were to be found Leicester, Florence and Saragossa; under Taurus, Dublin, Leipzig and Palermo. Gemini was the sign of Bruges and Cordova; Cancer was that of York, Constantinople, Rimini and Milan. Leo ruled Bristol and Prague, while Virgo ruled Paris, Heidelberg and Norwich. Antwerp,

Vienna and Lisbon were ruled by Libra, and Scorpio was the sign of Dover, Messina and Newcastle. Sagittarius ruled Avignon, Cologne and Toledo, while Capricorn ruled Oxford and Brussels. Salzburg and Salisbury were under Aquarius; Worms, Seville and Lancaster under Pisces. All these cities were considered to have the characters of their signs. Oxford, for instance, had the tradition and formality of Capricorn; Leo ruled imperial Rome, and Cancer the canals of Amsterdam. London was presided over by Gemini: always dual in nature, between north and south of the Thames and East and West End, it is a focus of communication which reveals its ruling planet, as does its fame for commerce, banking, docks, publishing and museums. Even its native, the Cockney, exhibits the quick tongue and sharp wit of Mercury.

Countries too were ruled by signs, some according to the Ptolemaic scheme and others according to their date of statehood. Britain was Arian, but the English state came under Capricorn from the moment of William the Conqueror's crowning, at noon on Christmas Day 1066. From the horoscope of that moment the following characteristics emerge. With the sun in Capricorn, and in the ninth house of travel and expansion, the rule of law, but with an imperial base, was laid. The English love of tradition, political sense, phlegmatic temperament and pragmatism are Capricornian; so is the English respect for achievement and station. Stable and conservative, England is also resilient and practical. Both widely feared and admired as a nation, England has a hidden reserve shown by the position of the moon in Pisces, and the ascendant of Aries shows an aggressiveness if it has to fight. Capricornian longevity has been borne out by a nine-hundred-year history.

On a smaller scale, even houses and places had their fate according to the laying of the foundation stone. For obvious reasons different buildings were begun at the times most useful for their purpose: a fortress with the sun in Aries or Scorpio, a corn exchange with the sun in Gemini, and an imperial palace with the sun in Leo at mid-heaven. Anyone wishing to erect a court of law would choose Capricorn, and Taurus or Libra for a building to be famed for beauty, elegance and ease.

The correct time to begin enterprises was most important. Gian Galeazzo Visconti preferred to apply planetary influence rather than prayer to reinforce his policies, and Pope Julius II arranged to have his coronation at an astrologically advantageous hour. Many generals would not begin battles until signalled by their staff astrologers.

The theory behind these decisions was contained in judicial astrology. In this an astrological calculation was made to find the moment of most favour within a possible period so as to utilize the balance of celestial influences particularly suited to the purpose. For example, Saturn might be unfavourably aspected to Jupiter, which would thwart an expanding operation like opening an embassy; on the other hand, a ruler who wanted to suppress a rebellion would employ Saturn's constraint to his advantage. This would require the drawing up of several charts, because the moon, a crucial factor, changes sign every two days. No diplomat would sue for peace with the moon in Aries. He would wait until it was in Taurus or Gemini, and then it had to be well placed to the sun and other planets. The mundane houses also had to be taken into account; and this affected the time of day to be chosen. The elected chart, as it was called, was designed to solve the particular problem; all the aspects and positions had to be as advantageous to the client as possible. This often narrowed down to one time option, which of course the astrologer working for the opposition would try to eliminate. England's initial reluctance to meet the Armada was not entirely due to naval tactics. The sun was squared to Queen Elizabeth's moon, and it was not a good time to fight.

By the late Middle Ages it was recognized that most men could not go against the celestial tides, or rise above the general laws of the moon, Mercury and Venus, which governed natural rhythms. These were the vegetable and animal levels of mankind, held in the carnal cycle of birth and death. There were, however, those who did not live entirely within the natural world, or even in the general fate of communities. These men had fates of their own, truly individual existences that defied surrounding situations. Such people could be saints or sinners; what marked them was that they lived by their sun sign, that is, that whatever they did was according to their individual nature, good or evil. The great have this distinction: they are not swayed as lesser men are. The Greeks had called them heroes, for they had a rare courage or drive that separated them from their fellows. To thinking astrologers this gave a clue to the nature of fate, in that if a man followed his sun, related his life to his inner self, he was freed from the obscuring power of the moon in his horoscope. This idea was by no means new; it has occurred in all mystical traditions, although in different forms. Its significance to the philosophical astrologer was enormous, because when a man lived by his sun his whole horoscope altered in emphasis: all the planets now came fully into play. Mars became a disciplined ally and Saturn an adviser in understanding, so that the man acquired vision and determination beyond ordinary men. Thus it was that he could withstand or avoid disasters that others could not bear or did not foresee. His fate was assured. The great Renaissance physician Paracelsus was considered mad and an enemy to his profession, but he accomplished much for medicine. So did Leonardo da Vinci, another greater than his time. These men lived according to the sun in themselves. Other people of destiny, like St Joan, fulfilled a collective or national fate. Here were several sets of laws at work, each belonging to a different level of reality.

Some astrologers speculated that the stars could only 'incline' the soul and not compel it. Fate was therefore a prison from which the soul could escape and rise, even higher than the planetary angels, to reach the world of pure spirits. This theology never entered the mainstream of astrology, but it lay behind several mystical disciplines, such as the Rosicrucians, who used astrological symbolism. Such speculations were meaningless to most people, who are entirely subject to the natural world. Few concerned themselves with studying deeply, and only a handful of these saw that even astrology was a fraction of a larger pattern. The reality of the world beyond the zodiac was as remote to most astrologers as the sun of individual fate to purely natural men.

6 Zenith

By the time of the Renaissance, astrology had permeated all classes of European society. At the most ordinary level farmers used almanacs which recommended planting at certain phases of the moon – for instance, plants that bear fruit above the earth should be sown when the moon was waxing, and root crops only when the moon was low or below the horizon. This gave rise to tables that set out the month, day and hour propitious for each species. Timing was crucial, because occasionally there were only minutes to play with, in order to catch the new moon before it set, or the full moon as it rose. Some almanacs gave instructions on planetary factors as well: it was, for example, unwise to plant when Saturn was squared to the moon because it restrained growth – although when in trine it added stamina. These instructions were often diligently followed.

By the sixteenth century the study of the astrological relationship between the human body and the heavens had been developed to a high degree. First the doctor classified his patient according to humour: the fire zodiac signs were choleric, the air sanguine, the water melancholic and the earth phlegmatic. Next he looked for the afflicting planet in the patient's horoscope – because every disease was classified according to a sign or a planet. If the throat was infected, he might expect to find Mars in Taurus, which would indicate inflammation in the neck, throat or shoulders; likewise Mars in Libra afflicted by Saturn in Capricorn would produce kidney or hip trouble. Heart diseases were considered to be common in people whose birth charts showed either an afflicted sun or a malefic (Mars or Saturn) in Leo. The illness would occur subsequently at a period of great tension on the sun or Leo. For similar reasons, if Saturn was ill-aspected in Capricorn maladies of skin and bone arose, and if in Gemini constriction in the lungs. Different combinations of planets in certain signs were associated with certain syndromes. Syphilis in an individual with a Jupiter-Saturn conjunction in Scorpio, the zone of the sex organs, was not uncommon; if Mars was in opposition in Taurus, the doctor would look for a secondary syphilitic infection in the throat.

The presence of planets in this or that sign did not mean a person would be ill whenever the area was transited or aspected. It merely indicated that these were the areas most likely to express the strain if the body was pushed beyond its normal tolerance.

In the sixteenth century the prevailing theory was that man possessed not one but three bodies: an elemental or physical carcase, alive in the vegetable and animal sense; a sidereal or planetary body, the soul; and a body of luminosity, the spirit. The first two can be diseased from without, Paracelsus observed, by contagious infection or malignant planetary influence. Illness may also be generated from within by a negative emotion such as deep hatred, which causes the luminous body to be even more obscured by the coarser bodies it interpenetrates. In time, the carnal body ejects the poisons of the soul via illness. Here, in Paracelsus' doctrine, was a definition of psychosomatic disease.

The interacting system between man and the heavens was seen to work through these three bodies. The elements composed the carnal vehicle, the planetary substance the sidereal body, with the sun as the connecting principle with the spirit. The moon acted as the pulse-pendulum between the elemental and planetary worlds. As an inherently luminous body, the sun related directly with the zodiac, so that man had a connection with the stellar world. Such a viewpoint was normal in an age which saw man and creation as integrated reflections of each other.

As the scientists of the day drew on astrological theory, so the artists developed astrological themes. Paintings, frescoes and carvings brought astrology into town and country, public and private buildings. Literature freely used astrological motifs; Chaucer, Dante and later Shakespeare could use astrology because every educated man knew his sign and planet. The 'Seven Ages of Man', in Jaques' famous speech in Shakespeare's *As You Like It*, are based on the planetary periods of life.

All the world's a stage,
And all the men and women, merely Players;
They have their exits and their entrances,
And one man in his time plays many parts,
His Acts being seven ages. At first the infant,
Mewling, and puking in the nurse's arms:
Then, the whining school-boy with his satchel
And shining morning face, creeping like a snail
Unwillingly to school. And then the lover,
Sighing like furnace, with a woeful ballad
Made to his mistress' eyebrow. Then, a soldier,
Full of strange oaths, and bearded like the pard,
Jealous in honour, sudden, and quick in quarrel,
Seeking the bubble reputation
Even in the cannon's mouth: and then, the justice,
In fair round belly, with good capon lin'd,
With eyes severe, and beard of formal cut,
Full of wise saws, and modern instances,
And so he plays his part. The sixth age shifts
Into the lean and slipper'd pantaloon,
With spectacles on nose, and pouch on side,
His youthful hose well sav'd, a world too wide,
For his shrunk shank, and his big manly voice,
Turning again toward childish treble pipes,
And whistles in his sound. Last scene of all,
That ends this strange eventful history,
Is second childishness, and mere oblivion,
Sans teeth, sans eyes, sans taste, sans everything.

Babyhood, with its lunar moods, is followed by the high-pitched mercurial whine of a boy, continually distracted as he creeps to school. This period is followed by the age of Venus, with all the concerns of sensuality, beauty and love. Then comes the age of Mars, when youth changes into assertive manhood. This is followed by the period of Jupiter, an archetype of middle age. The sixth vignette, old age, is distinctly saturnine. The seventh and last scene is the dissolution of the elements before dispersal at death. It is interesting to note that the sun is not included when a man reaches his prime. This makes one think that Shakespeare may have been writing about men who do not live by their sun, who cannot rise above the wheel of purely carnal birth, growth, decay and death. Perhaps this was the implication in Hamlet's question 'To be or not to be'. Here a prince, that is a hero, would not live by his sun or true nature until it was too late. The consequence was the destruction of himself and all those involved in his fate.

Running parallel to the arts and sciences were metaphysical studies that utilized astrology. Magic used the planets and gods, the operation being to invoke the archetypes of the upper worlds to act on the worlds below or penetrate the inner realm of the sidereal body. No doubt real magicians produced marvellous events, but these occurred deep within the psyche or planetary body, so that only those who could perceive at that subtle level could see the manifestation. In some cases the planetary gods might even appear in projected form, but such an experience was not recommended to the unprepared. To invoke the archetype of Mercury might cost a magician his sanity, the force of Venus his health, and the power of Mars his life. For this reason a long and disciplined apprenticeship was required.

Another tradition that used astrological principles was alchemy, itself as ancient as astrology. Alchemy, like magic, uses external symbols to describe a psychological operation. Almost invariably mistaken for primitive chemistry, it used the metals associated with the planets to hide from a hostile Church the real purpose of its work, which was the refinement of the soul. In broad principle, lead (Saturn) was the coarse base material of one's carnal nature, and gold (the sun) the refined incorruptible metal of the spirit. Silver was related to the moon, the ever-reflecting ego, quicksilver to the mercurial part of the psyche, copper to Venus and the instincts; iron was the discipline of Mars, and tin the jovian counterbalance of mercy. There were many complex combinations; but all alchemists, except those who thought that their purpose was actually to change lead into gold, were concerned with working the three-chambered retort of the elementary, sidereal and luminous bodies. On the strictly astrological side such delicate operations needed just the right planetary conditions, so charts were elected by the alchemist to match himself to a particular experiment. Astrological traces still remain in chemistry in the use of planetary symbols for metals.

On the purely occult side, chiromancy, the study of the hand, employed an astrological vocabulary, as did physiognomy, the study of the face. Both these arts argued that they too were the reflections of universal principles, but they never obtained the mass of data, or the comprehensive philosophy, possessed by astrology. In times of astrology's discredit both these and many other occult subjects were lumped together as pseudo-sciences, which in its pure form astrology never was.

The seeds of the decline of astrology lay in its very success. Anything and everything was related to it. Nothing could be considered without its influence. An example of this is in the image of Queen Elizabeth I of England presiding as the Prime Mover, over a Ptolemaic scheme of the State as macrocosm. In this the divine right of monarchy acted as the guiding will governing all spheres of the body politic. Royal authority based itself on the principle that everything in the universe was in its proper place, obeying an absolute and unquestioned rule from above: the ranks of stones, plants, animals and men were eternally fixed. This very rigidity of view was a weakness, and the first celestial sign of this came when a brilliant star flared for seventeen months in 1572. Probably a supernova, it strained the Ptolemaic order by its sheer presence, as did the comet of 1577 which appeared in an unexpected part of the heavens. Such cosmic anarchy could not be ignored, even though the prediction that the conjunction of Mars, Saturn and Jupiter in 1588 indicated the major defeat of an empire had come true in the defeat of the Armada sent by Spain against England.

Astrology was at the height of its influence. There were court astrologers everywhere: Elizabeth I had John Dee, and Catherine de Médicis Nostradamus. Neither was popular, and churchmen regarded them as sorcerers. For obvious reasons the birth of a prince was of great significance. The fate of the child and therefore of the nation might be determined from the same horoscope. Cardinal Richelieu, a farsighted Capricorn, once took care to place an astrologer behind a curtain in order to get the precise moment of a royal birth. While Elizabeth I was intellectually interested as well as pragmatic in her use of astrology, many courts were ruled by pure superstition. Catherine de Médicis surrounded herself with both magicians and astrologers in order to manipulate her family's destiny. Here it must be clearly said that there is a difference between clairvoyance and astrological prognostication. One is a vision; the other an assessment which is based on as much (and as little) data as a modern weather forecast. Many astrologers do make predictions; others refuse because of the margin of error, and others again because they consider that it can undermine individual responsibility. A great deal depends on whether a man is living by the sun or moon of his horoscope, the laws of his individual fate or those of his carnal nature. This ancient debate is still in progress.

To offset the malefic effects and encourage the benefic influences of the planets, men have devised talismans since early times. These magical protectors are sometimes just parchments enscribed with planetary, angelic or spirit symbols to counterbalance or stimulate the powers above or below. In some cases the actual planetary metals related to particular gods are employed, so that a medallion of iron would be worn to attract the power of Mars, while gold would carry within it the inherent influence and benefit of the sun. In contrast, a talisman designed to reduce a planetary force might include the lead of Saturn. To focus a talisman's purpose the planetary signs or magic sigils would be engraved or cast at a specific time so that the maximum planetary power was crystalized in it. Alchemists maintained that both the planet and its metal were but the upper and lower manifestations of the same thing: one a celestial, the other a terrestrial expression of a single principle. The magician saw the identical principle in the planetary spirit that he evoked in the ritual which took him out of the carnal body and into the world of the soul or sidereal body, sometimes called the astral world. The astrologer regarded these principles as planetary inclinations working through the nature of a man. Symbols are the language of the psyche. They link the above and the below, the inner and outer. Talismans, magical operations and horoscopes were all devices to contain, evoke or express the immense power of the world of archetypes. When Philip II of Spain wore black to draw the influence of Saturn, he touched upon the resources of the unconscious. His grave and authoritarian rule of a great empire carries Saturn's mark, from the monastery-palace of the Escorial to the repressive instrument of the Inquisition.

7 Eclipse

The eclipse of astrology began long before the supernova of 1572, when Nicholas of Cusa, in the fourteenth century, speculated about an infinite universe of which the earth could not possibly be the centre. As a cardinal he kept his thoughts to himself, because such ideas were heretical. A century later Copernicus (1473–1543), a Polish astronomer, finding the motions of the planets unsatisfactorily explained by Ptolemy, envisaged a completely new view of the solar system, with the earth in the third orbit out from the sun at the centre. To avoid heresy his publisher said the idea was merely a device for calculations. To push man out of his exalted place and shake the angels from their hierarchies was a threat to a society already under strain from the Reformation. The orthodox burned Giordano Bruno for declaring the universe was boundless.

The significance of Copernicus' idea was missed for a while, though it was taken up by a Protestant, Tycho Brahe, who disagreed with Ptolemy but did not agree with Copernicus either because his system removed man from the centre of creation. He arranged a geocentric system in which the sun orbited, with its heliocentric complement of planets, beyond the sphere of the moon. This kept the earth in an acceptable motionless position. Brahe's assistant Kepler went further and dispensed with the ancient concept of perfect spheres. He speculated on elliptical orbits, refined on Pythagorean geometry, and worked out specific musical tones for each planet which he based on the orbital velocities. All these investigations were part of a new outlook. The old criteria were being doubted; classical authority was being proved inaccurate by practical experiment. A world's end, which had been predicted for the year 1524, was coming true, but not in the way people expected.

Astrology during this period was at its high noon. Indeed, Brahe, Kepler and even Galileo practised it, although with varying degrees of commitment. No major developments occurred in the art itself, except that men like Robert Burton and Nicholas Culpeper collected interesting physiological and psychological data.

Culpeper was a seventeenth-century doctor who, like his predecessor Paracelsus, was particularly interested in herbal-astrological diagnosis and treatment. After an examination of the patient and his horoscope he applied the herbs sympathetic to certain planets as remedies for the diseases caused by their opposites. For example, certain afflictions of the liver, ruled by Jupiter, were neutralized by plants under Mercury. Culpeper further maintained that each plant was under the jurisdiction of a zodiac sign. Nettles were the plants of Aries, and useful for sore throats. Rhubarb acted as a mild Arian purgative; while elder flowers, a Taurian plant, when boiled in water made sunburn cool. The caraway of Virgo assisted digestion; and myrtle, under the same sign, relieved diarrhoea. Scorpio worked through broom and furze to clean chest and kidneys. Diseases of the skin were checked by the herbs of Saturn, such as knapwort, a marsh weed which acted as an astringent. The comprehensive list took years to compile, and Culpeper wandered all over England collecting and classifying his finds. Meticulously he would describe the plant and the conditions in which it was found, its time of flowering, its zodiacal ruler and the diseases it could cure. Behind the work was a deep feeling for the interrelation of the macrocosm, nature and man.

Burton was a scholar, and his contribution to astrology was a collection of observations on mental illness. In his work *The Anatomy of Melancholy*, he notes that Saturn and Jupiter in conjunction in Libra incline the subject to mild melancholia, while Saturn and the moon in conjunction in Scorpio make for severe melancholia. In both cases the constraint of Saturn is apparent. The milder condition is because of the expansiveness of Jupiter, the more severe because of the moon, which as ruler of Cancer is opposed to Saturn the ruler of Capricorn. The inturning moon is reinforced by Scorpio, so that in modern definition the person has a strong introversion. In contrast, Mars and the moon in conjunction, with Saturn and Mercury in opposition, produce a manic condition. This is generated by the stimulus of Mars and the excitability of Mercury in unfavourable aspect to the moon and Saturn. Each sign has its particular psychological affliction. Gemini and Libra generate schizophrenia, while Cancerian maladies make the patient retreat from the outer world. Leonine madness breeds megalomania, and Scorpio monomania and suicide.

The remedy for mental disorders was not as simple as for bodily ailments, for the problem by definition involves the sidereal body or psyche. The health of the soul is to a degree a matter of choice. As Burton's contemporary Sir Thomas Browne said, 'Burden not the back of Aries, Leo or Taurus, with thy faults'. To accept that one's horoscope utterly determines one's life is to believe oneself entirely a victim of circumstances. This is not the case, except for the mad, who withdraw into the moon's sphere between body and soul, to orbit in waxing and waning lunacy.

The issue of choice has always been a major one in astrology. Man has choice as his birthright, although most people do not make use of it. To have a bad horoscope need not necessary to a curse: many people with inharmonious aspects have made a success both of their inner and outer lives. Indeed, as Burton pointed out, squares and oppositions often generate energy and resilience, while the well-aspected, who lack tension, frequently collapse in setback and trial. This led in the seventeenth century to a reversed view of fortunate and unfortunate horoscopes; what did not change was choice. Two men in identical situations can have quite different attitudes. One may regard a cell as a prison, another as a quiet place of contemplation. Both perhaps have the sun and Mercury in the twelfth house, one becoming a habitual criminal, the other a retiring scholar. The option is open, not only to develop the talents indicated by the chart, but to turn the whole life into the luminous expression of the inner sun. Here lies the key to the prison of Fate, that is, those planetary laws that bind the soul.

On the more mundane side of astrology various branches continued the art of prediction. This could be done either by examining a natal chart in relation to the future positions of the planets or by progressing the sun round the horoscope, one degree for each year. Both were complex operations. An example of the first is the history of England, where Saturn in Aries always brings trouble. Astrologers recorded rebellion and pestilence in 1408, 1439 and 1554 – all transits of Saturn through England's rising sign. Saturn was there again in 1643 during the Civil War, and in modern times during the Blitz. However, disaster is not automatic, because other planetary factors may affect Saturn, increasing or diminishing its power. The same is true for individual horoscopes.

In progressing a horoscope, if the sun is moved thirty degrees, then the thirtieth year of that person is considered. After analysing all the new aspects made by the sun to the original chart, the progressed positions of the moon and planets have to be reviewed. Here complexity begins. For instance, a progressed sun may unfavourably aspect Mars in the house of partners. This could mean a domestic crisis in that person's thirtieth year. However, even without the possible mitigating effects of a progressed Jupiter, which may alleviate the conflict, the event might be useful or useless, depending on the person. It might work out as a surprise. One astrologer foresaw his own death at thirty-five, but the dying that occurred was that of a way of life. An intriguing phenomenon recorded down the ages is that of astrological twins, that is two people born virtually at the same time and place. The most famous case is of two men born in the same English parish. Both took over their fathers' businesses in the same month, married on the same day, fathered the identical number of boys and girls, were ill at the same time, suffered the same accidents, and died within an hour of each other. One was Samuel Hennings, an ironmonger, the other King George III.

Horary astrology was the answering of questions by erecting a chart based on the moment the question occurred. Thus, when a ship was overdue, it was considered possible to enquire into its fate because the celestial conditions generating the situation prompted the question. In the analysis the position of the planets in the houses would be crucial. If the sun was in Pisces, and also in the house of death, and badly afflicted, the conclusion was not encouraging. A similar method was used for medical prognosis. Occasionally the practice was used to solve crime, the time of the offence giving a horoscope which reconstructed the circumstances, including a description of the criminal. The validity of the technique is questionable; but it is worth recording that one Astronomer Royal did find a lost object by the method, to see if it worked. For obvious reasons the practice could be corrupted, so there was a rule that if Saturn was in the seventh house the question or the astrologer was suspect.

In 1582 the Julian Calendar (established by Julius Caesar in 46 BC) was updated by Pope Gregory XIII. This modification marked the official beginning of the end of classical authority. While the ordinary man worried about losing the deleted dates from his life, the more educated saw the old universal order start to crumble. The *coup de grâce* came when Galileo turned his telescope skywards and pierced the sublunary sphere to view the mountains and plains of the moon and the satellites of Jupiter. One glance through the telescope, and a whole cosmology was blown away. The Establishment fought to preserve the hierarchy of heaven that gave them power, by trying Galileo for heresy, but that did not invalidate what could be seen with one's own eyes. Through the telescope the sun was not an unblemished disc of purity, and Saturn had curious wings. After the sight of the moon's craters and mountains, who could believe in Ptolemy's universe? The gods were dead. Within the space of a few decades, men who still believed in the world of planetary spheres and angelic choirs ceased to be taken seriously. Astronomy, the physical sister of astrology, became the fashion. Every man wanted to study the sky, see what new marvels lay in a heavenly vault freed from mythology, superstition and scholarly creed. Astronomy quickly cut its family connection. Astrology was cast out by the rising authority of scientific reason.

No longer respectable, astrology retreated into obscurity. It was practised only by charlatans, and by a number of gifted amateurs who enjoyed it as an intellectual pastime. One of these was Elias Ashmole, the founder of the Oxford museum. However, despite its lost reputation, which made it a butt for satirists like Jonathan Swift, it did have champions in great men like Sir Isaac Newton, who, during a discussion on astrology, reprimanded a disparaging astronomer with the remark 'The difference between you and me, Mr Halley, is that I have studied the subject and you have not'. Newton was a deeply religious man and still saw the universe as an interconnected whole. Without this outlook he might never have conceived his theory of gravity, which describes, in terms of physical laws, the interaction of all the bodies in the universe. As a man who appreciated the old world-picture as well as the new physics, he has been called the last of the magicians and the first representative of the Age of Reason.

8 Re-emergence

Astrology remained in eclipse for almost two centuries. Traces of it were in the language – such as people being called saturnine, martial, or mercurial – but few seriously practised the art. However, the real threat to the system came with the detection of a new planet, Uranus, in 1781. This shook astrology even more profoundly than the Copernican reformulation. A complete reappraisal was needed. By the time of the discovery of Neptune in 1846, the situation was different. Astrology had begun to re-emerge, partly as a reaction against mechanical astronomy and partly through the stimulus of interest in the new planets.

Over a period of observation it was concluded that certain effects credited to the old gods actually belonged to the new. Thus sudden changes were ascribed not to Mars but to Uranus, which appeared to take up a trigger position in a planetary configuration. Neptune's operation was less dramatic: its very long period effected slow changes. Conclusions about the planets were based both on individual and mass responses to cosmic fluctuations. For example, in 1848 a series of domestic upheavals convulsed many countries, and between 1830 and 1900 seventy-five millions migrated from Europe. The two world wars had the same cosmic quality. No doubt every combatant and every migrant saw his role as personal choice, but hindsight indicates a global tension in which millions died and whole empires were destroyed. Here began a new branch of astrological study.

By the late nineteenth century astrology had re-established itself, but with a strong spiritual basis. For example, the Oriental idea of rebirth was incorporated, in that each person's chart indicated the lesson conveyed by his current incarnation. This concept was to give a new dimension to astrology. Much work was done in this field by the Theosophists, who saw astrology as a study of Karma and free will.

While the spiritual side of astrology progressed, the empirical aspect developed in the light of statistical method. Horoscopes were collated by the thousand and then classified by profession. From this certain patterns emerged. Farmers, for example, had a high

Saturn/moon relationship in their charts, while politicians invariably showed strong sun, Uranus or Jupiter emphasis. Studies of earthquakes revealed that Uranus was, in most cases, directly at mid-heaven over the site. One investigator, recognizing the build-up of the planetary configuration for an earthquake, predicted it would occur on 10 March 1933. It happened at Long Beach, California, on the day, killing 115 people. Naturally, astrologers published their findings, but orthodox science rejected the evidence, even though it had been arrived at empirically. As one scientist remarked: 'Even if it is true I cannot afford to believe in it.' Professional status came before truth.

On the psychological side astrology aroused great interest. Jung saw its validity, and many open-minded psychoanalysts began to use it. In their clinics ancient ideas began to surface again: the psychological archetypes that inhabit and influence the unconscious were matched to the gods. Thus the moon reflects the ego image of personal consciousness, Mercury the principle embodied in the archetype of the trickster, Venus the maiden in dreams, Mars the heroic element in the psyche, and Jupiter the generous, kingly image of our subconscious. Saturn embodies the essence of the Great Mother, the anima; and the remote progenitor, Uranus, embodies the powerful image of the father archetype, the magician or animus. These Jungian archetypes, expressed in dreams or projected on to other people or into life in general, represent the same principles as are embodied in the astrological gods. Moreover, the three divisions within man, of body, heart and mind, correspond to pairings of the gods: Mercury and Venus as the physical principles, Mars and Jupiter the emotional balances, and Saturn and Uranus the intellectual governors. The moon is a man's outer persona, the sun his inner individuation; all the planets together make up the collective unconscious.

Working separately from astrology, physical science was also coming to some old conclusions. Since Newton's time the sun had been watched closely and its sunspot rhythm recorded. This had by the nineteenth century been related to the fluctuating height of lakes, varying magnetic and auroral activity, and the eleven- to thirteen-year cycle of plants, as seen in tree rings and the quality of wines. This was the first observable connection science made between events in the heavens and occurrences on earth. With the discovery of the electromagnetic spectrum and the table of elements yet more interrelation between the terrestrial and celestial worlds was noted. With the advent of Einstein and of atomic physics, the purely mechanical view of the world was as shattered as Ptolemy's had been. Suddenly advanced physics had to be concerned with the metaphysical problems of philosophy. Earth and heaven met once more.

On the more mundane level the scientific appreciation that nature was composed of an ecological pyramid restated the ancient idea of degrees of reality: the food chains were hierarchically stepped, with man at the top of the mineral, vegetable and animal ladder. This web of organic life formed a ten-mile thick biosphere over the surface of the earth, which is itself delicately balanced in a crucial temperature zone between the orbits of Venus and Mars. By the time man landed on the moon it was known that the earth was surrounded not only by water and air but by an electromagnetic field. Here were earth, water, air and radiation or fire. Further, there was no such thing as empty space. Solar winds, cosmic rays, gravity, filled the void, as did a whole new universe discovered by the radio telescope. This new instrument revealed unseen stars and radio constellations, flooding the earth with radiations, as well as the fact that the sun fluctuated in size and rhythm and Jupiter emitted radio signals. Pythagoras's music of the spheres was not a poetic dream; nor was the ladder of creation that is slowly re-emerging. Science was retracing the steps of the thinkers it had mocked. Today, more and more, the connection between the heavens and the earth is being substantiated, be it in the clinical appreciation that blood coagulates faster at certain moon phases or in the discovery that the gross national product fluctuates with the sunspot and radio cycle. While not called astrology, all these conclusions nevertheless follow its basic maxim: 'as above so below'.

At the present time astrology has entered a popular boom. Beneath the revival of the traditional approach, much serious work is being done to bring astrology into the twentieth century. The new planet Pluto is being watched, and wider statistical surveys are being correlated, as well as the study of biological-lunar rhythms and psychological and planetary correspondences. More important, however, is the original point that astrology is again becoming a self-study. No amount of information will grant understanding and wisdom. Real knowledge is to see that contained within a man are the elements, the moon, sun, planets and stars. These are not mere celestial bodies but universal principles, expressed in the macrocosm as they are in us, the microcosm. When the monochord of creation is struck it vibrates in force and form, resounding through greater and lesser worlds until like instruments we reverberate in the finest vibrations and smallest particles that compose our being. We cannot but respond, for we are made in the identical image of the universe and its maker. Astrology is one among many traditions that enable us to know ourselves because that self is the Self, the Created and the Creator.

1 To early man the solar eclipse was an awesome sight. For a while the rhythms of the world were out of joint as the power of Heaven's brilliant ruler was diminished. Even the Earth cowered, with plants and animals stilled in a brief and false night. Such events were lodged in the folk memory. (Eclipse of the sun, Africa, 1973.)

2, 3 The ancient Egyptians saw the Milky Way as the body of the goddess Nut, bending over the sky. To other cultures it was a celestial road, or a stream of discarnate souls. All early peoples saw the universe symbolically, every force and form personified in a distinct entity. Thus Melich-pak, king of Babylon, presents his daughter to a godly being acting for the sun, moon and Venus (seen above in the upper world). The favours of these celestial powers were vital in peace and war. (Goddess Nut, relief, Egyptian; Relief, Babylonian, 13th c. BC.)

overleaf   4 Sky-oriented temples are found throughout the world. In them crucial points of the year were plotted by structural alignments, the axis of solstice and equinox determining the focus of the building and the time of the festival. Most temples were dedicated to the sun or moon, but more observant communities acknowledged the planetary rhythms and deities. (Winter sunset at Stonehenge, England.)

5, 6 The evolution of the zodiac took many centuries. First recognized as the
astronomical path of the sun through the constellations, its sections were given
symbols to illustrate the seasons of the year in detail. In an agricultural economy
where no one could ignore the sky, the signs became an integral part of the culture.
On the boundary stone to the left Scorpio appears, and above the whole zodiac is
seen on a coin of the classical period. Indeed, by Roman times the body of knowledge, once the exclusive property of the priests, ranged from metaphysics among
the philosophers to ignorant superstition in the market-place. These opposing poles
were to bring credit and discredit to astrology over the centuries. (Boundary stone,
Babylonian, *c.* 1120 BC; Zodiac coin, Greek Imperial.)

7, 8 All planetary gods are symbolic diagrams of cosmic principles. Based on observation, speculation and revelation, each image with its myths explains in archetype and allegory the laws embodied in the god. This is the language of pre-rational science, and of the unconscious of humanity. The sun and moon are celestial father and mother, and the male and female counterparts of nature: Apollo, on the left, is the active manifestation of power, Artemis one of the symbols for the full but passive force of the macrocosm. In the microcosm of man, both represent the same principles in the body and psyche, and as such resonate and respond to events in the world above. (Apollo in chariot, mosaic, Roman, AD 225; Artemis of Ephesus, marble, Roman, 2nd c. AD.)

Sapientia edificauit sibi domum.

9 The ancients' view of the Universe was hierarchical. They saw it rise from Hades up through the elements and planets to the Olympians, who, as six males and six females, expressed the positive and negative forces operating the Universe. In this engraving of the Graeco-Roman scheme the different planetary levels are shown, with Saturn's sphere contained by the zodiac. As the rulers of the planetary zone, the seven planetary gods, those of the moon, Mercury, Venus, sun, Mars, Jupiter and Saturn, exerted the major influence. (Graeco-Roman Universe, from Catharis' *Immagini degli Antichi*.)

10 With the reason of Aristotle and the revelation of Plato came a subtle appreciation of the different levels of experience. In this medieval, Christianized version, the ladder of consciousness is set out in stones, plants and stars as well as angels, men and animals. The notion of a continuum of existence, with no break, formed the basis of astrology. Every body and every mind was influenced by everything, although the greater always ruled the lesser. (Celestial ladder, from Raymond Lull's *De Nova Logica*, 1512.)

11, 12 The planetary gods are poetic analogies of celestial and psychological functions. Whereas the sun and moon *(pls. 27–28)* express inner and outer human consciousness, the planets describe the operational principles of action, heart and mind. This view reflects the concept of the solar system of the psyche, in which the instincts, emotion and thought, orbit the luminaries of the self and ego. In our example the disciplined Etruscan Mars illustrates the original image of the war god as controlled emotion, quite contrary to the degenerate picture of him in later times. The mosaic of Venus, in contrast, expresses the active instinctual desire for pleasure and revulsion against discomfort. (Mars, bronze, Etruscan, 5th c. BC; Venus, mosaic, Roman, 3rd c. AD.)

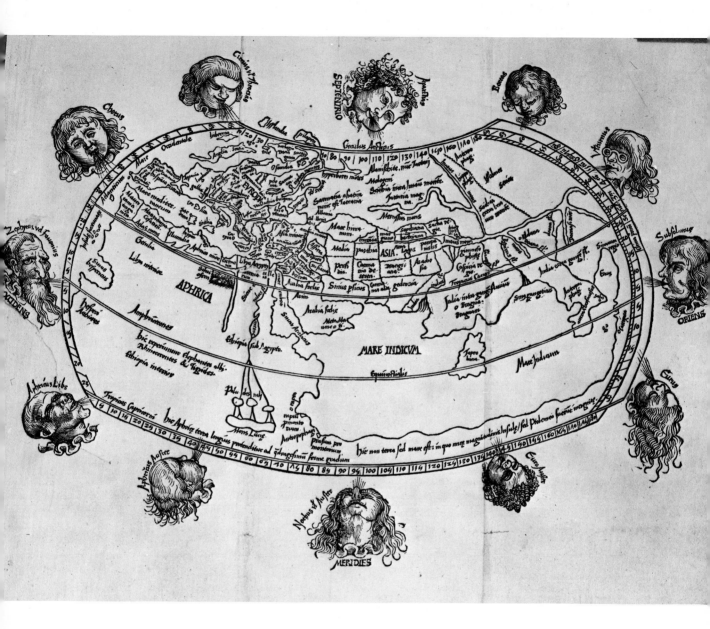

13 Western astrology owes much to the Greek-Egyptian scholar Ptolemy, of the second century AD, who compiled a work on all the available data on astrology. Besides being a geographer and compiler of a map of the known world (of which the illustration is a later copy), he assigned zodiacal rulership to countries. In this scheme Britain was under Aries, Gaul and Italy under Leo, India Capricorn, Spain Sagittarius and Egypt Gemini. This last country still exhibits the sign's twin nature in its division into Upper and Lower Egypt, and in the mercurial loquacity and wit of the people (Mercury being the planetary ruler of Gemini). Ptolemy's own city, Alexandria, had the world's first museum and library (communication being an attribute of Mercury and of Gemini). (Ptolemaic world, map from Gregor Reisch's *Margarita Philosophica*, AD 1503.)

The diagram contains the following labels, from center outward:

Hemphta

Numen Triforme et παντόμορφον

Inner houses (Dodecamorion seu Domus):
- I — Dodecamorion, seu, Prima domus seu mansio — Capricornus — Anubis
- II — Dodecamorion, seu Domus — Aquarius — Canopus
- III — Dodecamorion, seu Domus — Pisces — Ichton
- IV — Dodecamorion, seu Domus — Aries — Amun
- V — Dodecamorion, seu Domus — Taurus — Apis
- VI — Dodecamorion, seu Domus — Gemini — Hercules et Apollo
- VII — Dodecamorion, seu Domus — Cancer — Hermanubis
- VIII — Dodecamorion, seu Domus — Leo — Momphta
- IX — Dodecamorion, seu Domus — Virgo — Isis
- X — Dodecamorion, seu Domus — Libra — Omphta
- XI — Dodecamorion, seu Domus — Scorpius — Typhon
- XII — Dodecamorion, seu Domus — Sagittarius — Nephte

Outer ring numbered 1–36.

14 In this seventeenth-century engraving the blending of cultures is seen in the Latin, Greek and Egyptian versions of the zodiac. This process occurred throughout astrology's development, each phase adding its own findings and understanding (as with the thirty-six decans round the edge of the diagram), until the study became so complex that it was a full-time profession. This gave rise to the best and worst practitioners. In Rome, for example, emperors would consult their Chaldeans, as astrologers were called, on policy, while having to drive out the charlatans who defrauded their more gullible subjects. (Hieroglyphic plan of the ancient zodiac, from A. Kircher's *Oedipus Aegyptiacus*, 1653.)

15 Ptolemy's *Tetrabiblos* preserved the body of astrological knowledge through the eclipse of classical learning. In this Byzantine image nothing has been altered or added for hundreds of years, because Ptolemy's word was considered to be the final authority; to advance further, astrology had to wait for the Arabs. (Helios (sun) with signs of zodiac, from Ptolemy's *Astronomy*, Byzantine, AD 820.)

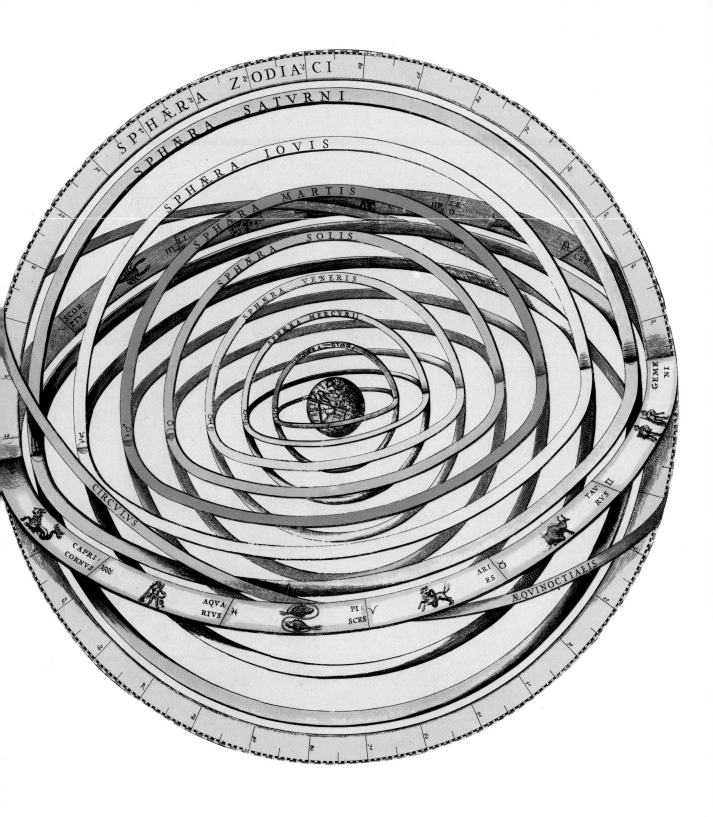

16 The Ptolemaic Universe was based on direct observation and philosophical conception. Thus Saturn, the most remote planet to be seen with the naked eye, was embedded in the crystalline sphere next to the zodiac. The whole scheme was based on perfect geometry and balance, only the sublunary world being subject to change and decay. (Orbits of the planets, engraving by A. Cellarius, 1668.)

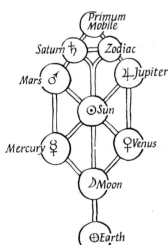

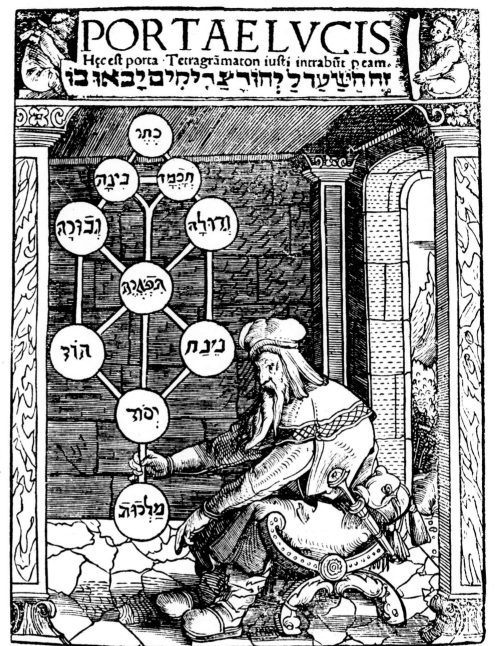

17 Jewish interest in astrology is evident in the Talmud and Kabbalah. Indeed, Kabbalists placed the planetary gods on the diagram of the Tree of Life, saying that they expressed in mythological and astronomical parallel the qualities of the Divine emanations or Sephiroth whose relationships the Tree defines. In this presentation, the active (right) and passive (left) roles of the planets are defined, as is the central line of consciousness in the luminaries (sun and moon). (Tree of Life, engraving from Ricius' *Portae Lucis*, 1516.)

18 The Christians (and the Jews) officially banned astrology, considering God the only ruler of destiny. However, despite resistance to heathen ideas, astrology did influence the early Church in the association of the symbols of the Evangelists with the fixed cross of the Bull, the Lion, the Man (of Aquarius) and the Eagle, Scorpio's alternative symbol (Revelation 4:7; see pp. 126–7). (Symbols of the Evangelists, page from *Book of Kells*, Celtic, c. AD 800.)

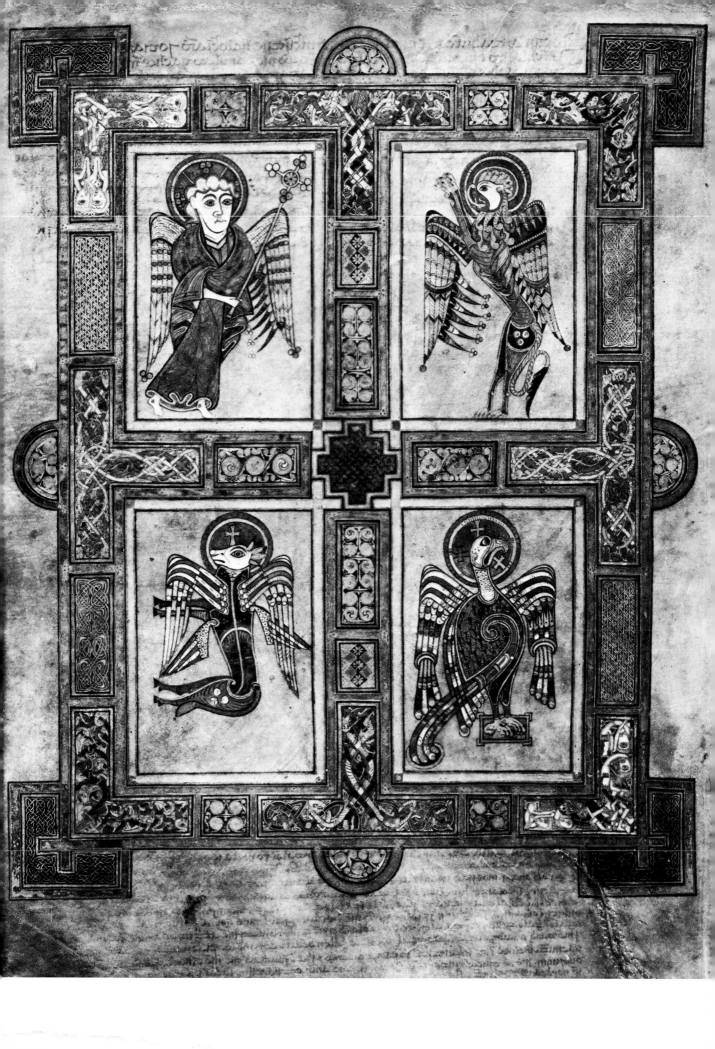

19 The Arabs picked up the development of astrology where the Greeks had left off. As the atmosphere of learning revived, enquiry and investigation brought the study to life. Nor was this interest purely academic. As in Mesopotamia, Greece and Rome, astrology permeated into general life to influence the public and domestic scene. (The zodiac, plate, Persian, signed Abd al-Wahid, dated AH 971 : AD 1563–4.)

20 The Arabic love of subtle detail had full range in astrology. While, for example, the Greeks had contemplated the geometric relationships between planets, the Arabs investigated the more delicate nuances of the relationships of the archetypes to one another in the light of varying conditions. Here the moon and Jupiter meet in Sagittarius. (Page from MS. of Abu Ma'shat, Islamic, Cairo, c. 1250.)

21 The moment of birth determines the nature of a person, as the ever-changing planetary situation is crystallized in the body. From that moment the soul is fixed in a particular psychological configuration which will express the life of the individual temperament. The positions of the heavenly bodies are crucial; but they are only indicative of the conditions in the subtle realm from which the soul emerges. This is why the astrologers observe the sky when the child is born. (Moment of birth, woodcut, 1587.)

22 Out of the Arabs' study of the moment of birth came the mundane house system. In this the anatomy of the psyche, as mirrored in the planets in the zodiac, is seen in relation to the way the same nature manifests itself to the outside world *(mundus)*: hence the name 'mundane'. With this innovation greater clarity could be achieved both in the interpretation given to the client and in the understanding of the astrologer. The engraving sets out the departments of life credited to each house. (Mundane houses, woodcut, from Georg Peurbach, 1515.)

ISTI MIRANT STELLA

23 Comets have never played a major part in astrology, but as periodic visitors to
the earth they were always considered disturbers of the regular rhythms of the
planets; this gave them the reputation of foreshadowing changes. This image was
enhanced by their appearance, which was seen as a fiery sword in the heavens.
(Halley's Comet in 1066, Bayeux tapestry, Norman, 12th c.)

24 By the Middle Ages astrology had entered the West. St Thomas Aquinas, in the scholastic version of Ptolemy's scheme, still placed the elemental world at the centre of the planetary spheres, but with nine orders of angelic beings above to replace the Olympians. This chain of living became part of the medieval outlook, and fostered the progress of astrology in Europe. (The Universe, fresco by Piero di Puccio, Campo Santo, Pisa, *c.* 1400.)

FLEGMAT   **SANGVIN**

JÆLANG   **COLERIC**

25 The Greek concept of the four humours relates to the seasonal states of cold, moist, hot and dry, and to the four elements and their zodiacal signs. These combinations fascinated scholastic astrologers, who with their new-found intellectual freedom could explore the metaphysics of the subject. Such studies helped the understanding of causal laws and the observation of effects. (Four humours, engraving from L. Thurneysser's *Quinta essentia*, 1574.)

26 One application of astrology came in medicine. Here the planetary situation was considered to have a direct influence on the soul and consequently on the body. After astrological diagnosis, remedies were applied to counter planetary pressures upsetting the balance of the humours or body fluids, with particular regard to the moon, which affected the crisis cycle of the disease. (Physician-astrologer, print from *Kalendertafel* by Hans Holbein, 1534.)

27 In astrology the sun represents the essence of a man's being. Its position in a horoscope is a prime factor, because the zodiac sign it is in indicates the nature of that essential self which will govern and shape the fate of the individual life. (Sun, miniature from MS. *De Sphaera*, Italian, 15th c.)

28 The moon in a birth chart depicts the ordinary mind, and its zodiac situation determines the kind of ego consciousness with which a man will view the world. As the moon reflects the sun, it acts within man as the *persona* or mask: the personality that overlies the true self. This is the sun–moon relation in a chart. (Moon, miniature from MS. *De Sphaera,* Italian, 15th c.)

✦ MERCVRIVS ✦

29 The chameleon quality of Mercury makes the planet take on whatever zodiac sign it is in and enhance it with intelligence. Moreover, if it is close to another planet in a chart it will adopt that planet's function and add a sharpness to it. Mercury represents the mutable aspect of a man's nature. (Mercury, miniature from MS. *De Sphaera*, Italian, 15th c.)

· VENVS ·

30 Venus, like all planets, may be well or badly aspected: that is, the angles between it and the other planets can intensify or retard its function. Thus, Saturn square (at right angles to) Venus, the archetype of instinct, acts as a constraint on the individual's desires; this produces, according to the other astrological factors involved, either asceticism or repression. (Venus, miniature from MS. *De Sphaera*, Italian, 15th c.)

31 The psychological principle of Mars is emotional control. However, in a sign which works to his detriment, like Libra, his martial decisiveness is split and he becomes dangerous. Like all planets, he is at his strongest in his own active sign; in Mars' case, this is Aries (see pp. 126–7). (Mars, miniature from MS. *De Sphaera*, Italian, 15th c.)

·IVPITER·

32 Jupiter, the complementary emotional planet to Mars, acts as the expansive counterpart to Mars' contraction. Further, each planet has both a masculine and a feminine role; Jupiter is active in Sagittarius and passive in Pisces. These emphases subtly affect the balance of a chart. (Jupiter, miniature from MS. *De Sphaera*, Italian, 15th c.)

· SATVRNVS ·

33 Saturn, the symbol of intellect, influences, as do the other planets, the mundane houses, so that his cool long-term view pervades whichever department of life is governed by the house in which he is at the hour of birth. Thus, he makes a man prudent in business if in the second house, or calculating in love if in the fifth. (Saturn, miniature from MS. *De Sphaera*, Italian, 15th c.)

34 All the planets are enclosed by the zodiac, which is itself part of the celestial sphere centred on the earth. The geocentric view is made yet more relative by the individual horoscope, which is nothing but a diagrammatic picture of the heavens seen at a given time and from a given spot on Earth. (Atlas holding up the world, woodcut, 1559.)

35 The zodiac is the gradual unfolding of the year. Here Mars, ruler of Aries, submits to Venus, goddess of Taurus. All about, spring is expressed in the plant, animal and human kingdoms. (April, painting by Francesco del Cossa, Palazzo Schifanoia, Ferrara, *c.* 1470.)

36 In Gemini, Venus' matching of pairs moves into the domain of Mercury, the patron of communication; and he completes the courtship through pollination. (May, page from MS. *Les Très Riches Heures du Duc de Berry,* French, early 15th c.)

Mercurius.

37 Each astrological planet is expressed in certain occupations. Here Mercury's principle manifests in skills of great dexterity, mental agility and cunning of hand. Cold and precise, the mercurial jobs have a deftness about them that requires an ephemeral and sometimes shallow intelligence. Their hallmark is speed and exchange, and their practitioners are easily recognized by an ever-moving focus of interest. (Mercury as patron of certain occupations, woodcut by Hans Sebald Beham, 1530–40.)

Venus.

38 Venus rules the arts. Pleasure is her métier. As the goddess of love, some unconventional jobs are hers. She also rules the care and the hunting of animals, as well as the cooking and eating of their flesh. She has a sensual approach, sometimes pleasant, sometimes the reverse. (Venus as patroness of certain occupations, woodcut by Hans Sebald Beham, 1530–40.)

overleaf　39 Scorpio is the mid-autumn phase, the sign of death and regeneration. The sowing of seeds, as the natural winter death of nature approaches, symbolizes that aspect of man. In astrology every sign is present in every horoscope, although it may not be emphasized. The neutral signs affect the individual in a general way; thus, with Scorpio, we are all subject to death. (October sowing, Scorpio, from *Bedford Hours*, French, c. 1423.)

Mars.

40 The martial occupations are ones of discipline. Besides the arts of war, they include trades and professions requiring penetration and judgment. Traditionally butchers, surgeons, workers in iron, inventors, investigators and pioneers come under Mars. The qualities of such occupations are courage, control and decision, be it in a court cross–examination, a commando raid or a delicate surgical incision. (Mars as patron of certain occupations, woodcut by Hans Sebald Beham, 1530–40.)

41 The employments of Saturn are usually associated with building, farming, mining, indeed anything to do with the earth. Also included may be government, administration, law, and management of large enterprises. Philosophers and practical idealists are ruled by Saturn, who gives his occupations a stable, long-term set of criteria. His workers often have a powerful but prudent ambition. (Saturn as patron of certain occupations, woodcut by Hans Sebald Beham, 1530–40.)

42 By the late Middle Ages astrology had affected all levels of society. Farmers and traders used simple woodcut calendars for planting and fairs, while the nobility had exquisite manuscripts such as the Duc de Berry's Book of Hours to illuminate the zodiacal year. (February, page from MS. *Les Très Riches Heures du Duc de Berry*, French, early 15th c.)

43 Zodiacal Man is a constant theme in medieval manuscripts. Here the signs are associated with corresponding principles in the body to show man, the most perfect creature in the world, as the microcosmic image of the heavens. As such, man himself reflects the celestial mirror. (Zodiacal Man, page from MS. *Les Très Riches Heures du Duc de Berry*, French, early 15th c.)

44 Investigation into the workings behind astrological traditions required both a factual and an inspirational approach. Only a few men, like Paracelsus, understood that beneath the physical appearance of things lay an invisible but real world of cosmic law. This realization was based on direct experience and insight, as our print depicts, into the next world, that is, the ever-present but subtle realm of existence which the soul inhabits. Such mystical appreciation confirmed that man possessed an organized body not unlike his carnal one, which was subject to planetary pressures. The dynamics of the sidereal body, as it was called, were studied in metaphysical astrology. (Scholar penetrating through the sky into the next world, engraving. Swiss, *c.* 1500.)

45 The Wheel of Fortune was a common astrological theme of medieval times. In this print Mars has his moment of ascendancy, but this will give way to the sun, followed by Venus. The wax and wane of planetary influence was fully appreciated in the tides of fortune for mankind, the wise and the enterprising catching and using the period of each god. For ordinary men there was little choice, because without real knowledge or a flair for timing they were subject to the mass ebb and flow that governs world affairs. Escape was possible from these events, but only if an individual really wanted to choose it. The same situation occurs today. (Wheel of Fortune, page from MS., German, c. 1490.)

46 The Church uses astrological motifs; and Pisces is a Christian symbol. It is also the sign of a 2,000-year period in the Great Year created by the precession of the equinoxes. The Age of Pisces was dominated by religion, our own Age of Aquarius by political and social ideas. (Pisces, stained glass, Chartres Cathedral, 13th c.)

47 The symbolic structure of astrology is reflected in much of European literature. Dante used it in his *Divine Comedy*, with Beatrice leading him up through the planetary spheres to the Empyrean Heaven of pure light. (Dante's Universe, painting by Domenico de Michelino, Cathedral, Florence, 1465.)

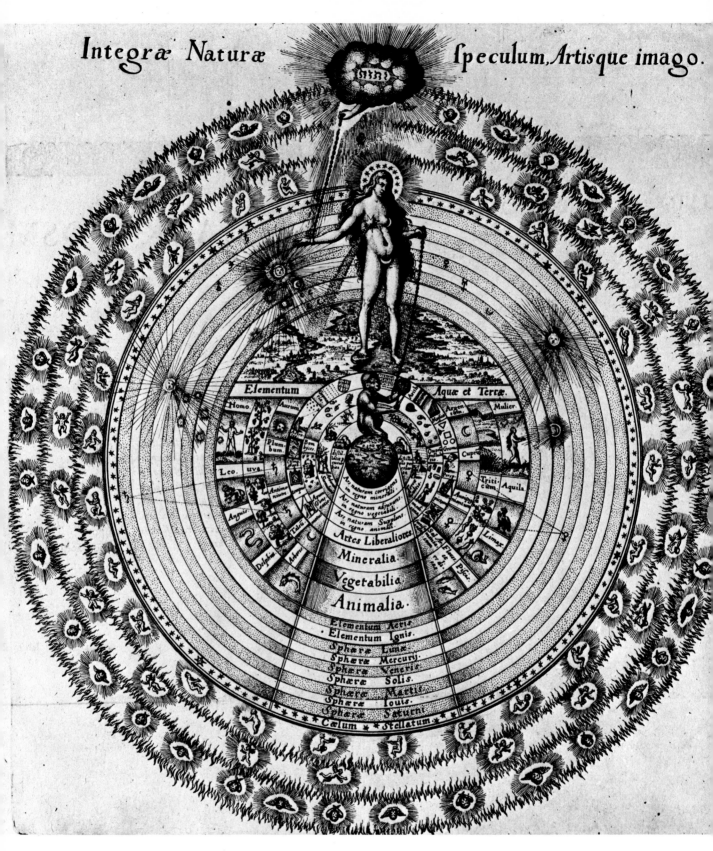

48 Kabbalist astrology shows three higher levels surrounding the world of stars, planets and earth. Everything is governed by angelic providence, while below, flanked by the mineral, vegetable and animal kingdoms, the monkey mind of sensual man tries to understand the universe. Above the World Mother manifests and transmits the will of God. The diagram well illustrates the outlook of thinking astrologers. (The World, engraving from Robert Fludd's *Utriusque Cosmi . . .*, 1617.)

SPHÆRA CIVITATIS

49 The symbolic power of astrology has always been strong. Here it is used to endorse an absolute monarch, the qualities of the planets and spheres enhancing the royal character, the celestial world supporting the anointed queen whom providence has placed on the English throne. Possessing the Divine Right of the Crown, Elizabeth could not but be the First Mover of the Realm, the highest power in her own little cosmos. (Elizabethan State, engraving, English, 16th c.)

50 Astrology was everywhere in Renaissance life. Its motifs were to be seen in domestic decoration. In this painting the celestial gods emanate the various arts, sciences, crafts and occupations that are associated with them. (Painted table-top, by Martin Schaffner, 1533.)

51 The knowledge of celestial influence also found its way into the garden; this ivory sundial is engraved with planetary hours. Such a clock not only told the time but indicated the god presiding over the moment. No lovers with this information would ever spoil their tryst by meeting under Saturn, but choose the hour of Venus. (Diptych sundial, ivory and gilt brass, German, 1618.)

52 The technology of astrology evolved over the centuries. Here is an astrolabe designed for setting up quick horoscopes. Each arm represents a planet that can be turned to the relevant zodiac position. From this all the angles can be seen at a glance and calculations for the timing of medical applications be made. Such instruments were as vital to doctors at one time as a stethoscope. (Astrological astrolabe, brass, European, *c.* 1450–1500.)

53 The armillary sphere is basically a teaching device. It demonstrates the celestial sphere and its various coordinates in relation to the earth at its centre. All good astrologers had to know their astronomical theory, so that their calculations could be accurate. It was said, however, that one could be *too* precise: matters of the soul do not have such hard edges as tools and theories. (Armillary sphere, brass, Italian, 1601.)

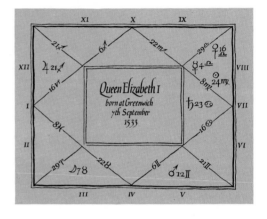

Queen Elizabeth I
born at Greenwich
7th September
1533

54 The horoscopes of rulers have usually been recorded, because their personal fates have a bearing on an entire nation. The Virgin Queen, Elizabeth, born under Virgo, did not have the title only by virtue of her sun sign. With Saturn in Cancer in the House of Partners, delay in marriage might be expected, especially with Mars in Gemini in the fifth house. This divides emotional decisions, creating frustration. Moreover, sun squared Jupiter in two houses of secrets (the eighth and twelfth) indicated a difficult personal life, although a Capricorn ascendant gave her outward authority. This temperament left its mark on English history. (Queen Elizabeth I, miniature by Nicholas Hilliard, English, late 16th c.)

55 Alchemy, the spiritual cousin to astrology, ran parallel in development. Often it borrowed the symbols of astrology to describe in its terms the archetypes of alchemical metals which also represented psychological principles. Gold was the terrestrial sun; and it was the alchemists who gave quicksilver the name of Mercury. To transform lead (or base consciousness) into gold (enlightenment) the concurrence of the macrocosm was vital. Alchemy directly utilized astrological techniques to choose the best time to begin an operation. The great work, alchemists said, should only be begun with the sun in Aries, Taurus or Gemini. (Page from MS. of Norton's *Ordinall*, English, 15th c.)

56 Magic draws on astrology because the spirits it seeks to evoke are the same archetypes that astrology defines. The secrets of real magic are scrupulously guarded; to arouse Venus or Mars in an unprepared psyche can be dangerous. Magic is quite separate from astrology. (Elementary world, engraving from *Museum Hermeticum Reformatum et Amplificatum*.)

57 In Sir Richard Burton's *Anatomy of Melancholy*, various maladies of the soul are described with their planetary aspects. Most of these observations are now no more than curiosities, but in time astrologers discovered more of the laws that govern the pressures in the psyche's structure. The sidereal body, it became apparent, was as subject to organizational disturbance as was the physical. (Title page from Richard Burton's *Anatomy of Melancholy*, 1628.)

THE
ANATOMY OF
MELANCHOLY.
What it is. With all the kinds causes,
symptomes, Prognostickes, & severall cures of it.
In three Partitions, with their severall
Sections, members & subsections.
Philosophically, Medicinally,
Historically, opened & cut vp.
BY
Democritus Junior.
With a Satyricall Preface, Conducing
to the following Discourse.
The thirde Edition, corrected and
augmented by the Author.
Omne tulit punctum, qui miscuit vtile dulci.

Zelotypia.

Democritus Abderites.

Solitudo.

Inamorato.

Hypocondriacus.

Superstitiosus.

Democritus Junior.

Maniacus.

Borago.

Oxford
Printed for
Henry Cripps.
1628

Helleborus.

58, 59 Two things brought about the eclipse of astrology. The first was Copernicus' notion of an objective solar system, replacing the earth-orientated Ptolemaic scheme with a helio-centric view; and the second was Galileo's telescope, which revealed the planets as bodies. Both innovations shifted people's interest towards a physical outlook on the Heavens. Astrology inevitably withered. (Copernican universe, engraving from *Atlas Coelestis* by A. Cellarius, 1660; Man looking at Saturn, panel of a triptych by Donato Creti, *c.* 1671–1749.)

60, 61 The rise of astronomy from the seventeenth century onwards overshadowed astrology. With better telescopes, the planets and stars were scrutinized, measured and mapped. There was an abundance of new theories about the universe beyond the discredited Ptolemaic world picture; and yet all were in a direct line of succession from its earth-orientated viewpoint. The orrery (below) epitomizes the whole tendency to interpret the universe in purely mechanical terms. Like the map of the moon seen here, the heavens had become arid. Astrology, the study of celestial moods, was redundant. (Orrery, 18th c.; Map of the moon, engraving by Riccioli, 1651.)

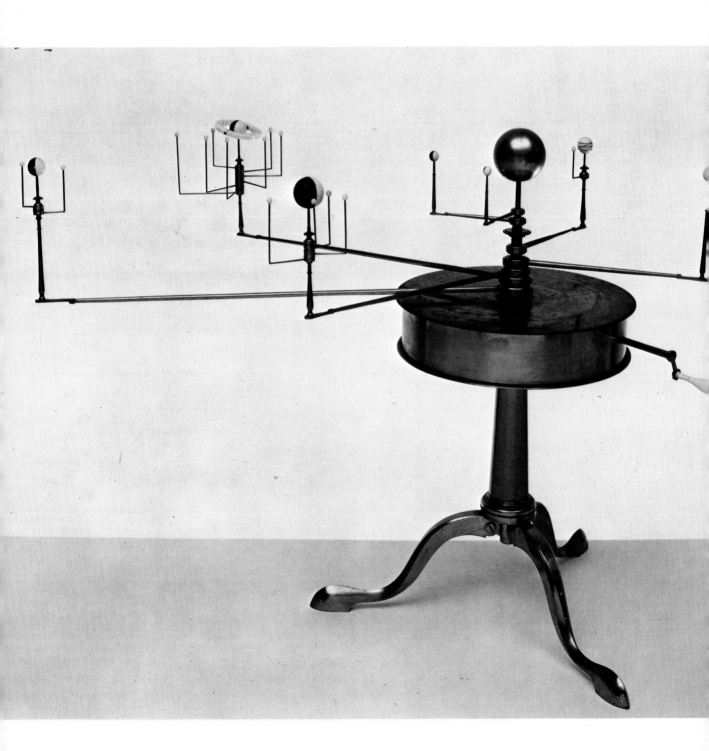

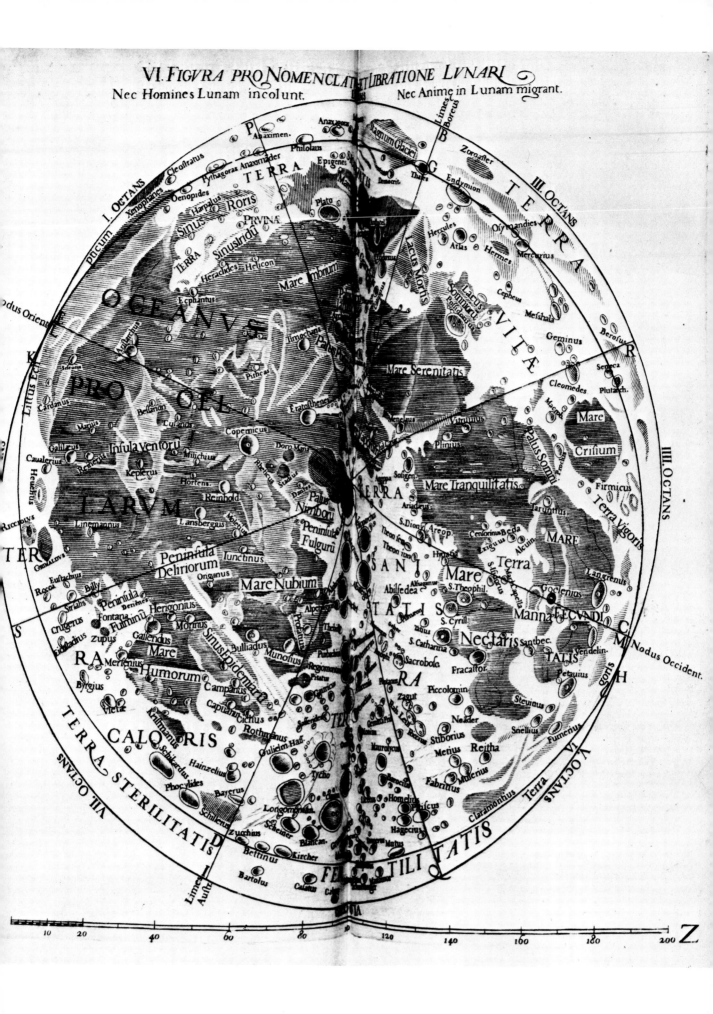

62 Today astrology is again a serious study. This is not only because of interest in things spiritual, but because science is gathering evidence of an integrated network of celestial, terrestrial and ecological relationships. These studies have revealed an interconnectedness not unlike the ladder of creation described in ancient traditions. Indeed, advanced physics and psychology are on the frontiers of philosophy and mysticism. With the Earth now seen as a whole and known to be influenced by galactic, stellar, solar and planetary forces, many astrological laws are being verified. Perhaps astrology will be honoured tomorrow, as it was in the past, by those who perceive no separation between Heaven and Earth. (Earth, from NASA Apollo moonshot.)

*Documentary illustrations
and commentaries*

Origins

The beginnings of astrology are unknown. All that can be guessed at is that its roots are in the first stable communities with a simple calendar and fixed sighting arrangements for observing the sky. As cultures developed, so did measuring techniques, records and speculative thought. From this a body of celestial and terrestrial constants emerged that formed the basis of astrology.

1 The sun was probably the first heavenly force to gain man's attention. All over the world temples were built in honour of his power and movement. This chariot of the sun from prehistoric Denmark is a recurring personification. (Sun chariot, bronze, Denmark, c. 1000, National Museum, Copenhagen.)

2 The ziggurats of Mesopotamia were not only temples but observatories, whose great height gave a wide field of view. This building technology, together with the remarkably clear air of the country, helped establish the Chaldeans as the leading astrologers. (Ziggurat of Ur, Mesopotamia, c. 2000 BC.)

3 This Babylonian tablet shows the disc of the sun between its deity and mortals. The sun was the physical manifestation of a celestial intelligence embodied in the god. (Tablet showing refoundation of sun temple, Sippar, Babylonia, 9th c. BC., British Museum.)

4 While the Hebrew seven-branched candlestick is usually regarded as a decoration, it is also a cosmic diagram of active and passive forces on either side of a central column of equilibrium. The seven lights express the same seven principles described in the planetary gods. Here metaphysics and design are one in symbolism, the technological language of the ancient world. (Menora, gilt glass, Byzantine, 4th c. AD, Israel Museum, Jerusalem.)

5 By Assyrian times astrological tools were quite sophisticated, as one can see by this astrolabe. Accuracy was achieved with the development of calibration based on the minute, hour, day, month and year. (Astrolabe, Assyria, 7th c. BC, British Museum.)

3

4

5

Classical world

The influence of astrology on the classical world was great and varied. It fascinated high and low, philosophers and fools. Imported from the East, its sense of order appealed to the Greeks, who rationalized and developed it as both a physical and a metaphysical study; astronomy and astrology were then considered the same.

6 The Pythagorean school considered the celestial bodies as living beings in precise relation to one another. This is seen in the musical Diaspon scheme of perfect harmonics, in which the earth, moon, planets, sun and stars occupy tonal positions. (From Stanley's *The History of Philosophy*.)

7 The Egyptians had developed their own zodiac, but in time it merged into the common tradition. The zodiac here is in the root of a temple whose axis points toward the heart of the Milky Way. (Zodiac of Denderah, engraving after relief of Ptolemaic period, 19th c., Louvre, Paris.)

8 This woodcut expresses well over a thousand years' respect for Ptolemy, the Greek-Egyptian astrologer of Alexandria. (Celestial sphere, woodcut by E. Schön, Germany, 1515.)

9 The study of the geometrical angles or aspects between signs and planets was a most important refinement. These described the fluctuations of stress within the general celestial tides. (Signs and aspects, woodcut, Germany, 16th c.)

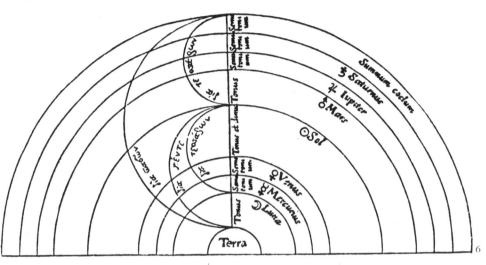

6

7

8

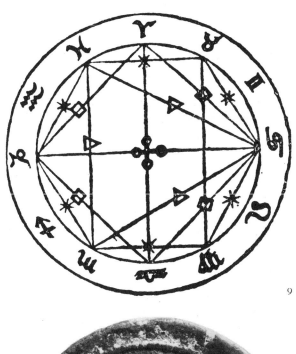

9

10–13 The ruler's birth sign was struck on coins to show the heavenly source of his authority. However, there were disadvantages: enemies could use an emperor's horoscope against him. Another danger was for the astrologer himself. Thrasyllus cleverly saved his life when Tiberius asked if he knew the hour of his own death. The astrologer, guessing the emperor intended to have him killed, replied 'Yes', adding that, because of similarities in their charts, the Emperor would only outlive him by a day. (Moon in Cancer, drachm of Antoninus Pius, Egypt, 2nd c. AD; Capricorn, denarius of Augustus, Rome, 1st c. BC; Jupiter in Sagittarius, Leo, drachms of Antoninus Pius, Egypt, 2nd c. AD; all British Museum.)

10

11

12

13

Early Jewish and Christian thought

The Jews and Christians were concerned with Heaven, but not the one of astronomy and astrology, although the Jews were acquainted with the studies in the culture they lived in. Both religions' prime interest was in revelation and theology, which only considered the Law: that of the world above mundane existence, or that of the conduct of men. The influence of pagan ideas was carefully buried beneath the terminology of orthodoxy.

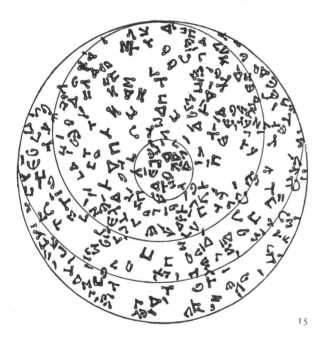

14 The vision that Ezekiel saw by the River Cheber consisted of four levels; the earth, the chariot, the throne and a man. This was an allegory of the Four Worlds of the Universe, later to be detailed in the medieval Kabbalah and to underlie astrological metaphysics. (Vision of Ezekiel, from the Bear Bible.)

15 According to the Kabbalah the stars may be seen as Hebrew letters in the sky. These can be read as words and statements on the future. However, whether this Jewish star map can be used in this way depends on the spiritual level of the interpreter rather than his knowledge of Hebrew.

16 An unusual star drew three kings to Palestine and came to culmination over Bethlehem in Roman times. Some astrologers say that this event was an exact conjunction of a large number of planets that gave the appearance of a single star. Astrologically a very propitious birth. (Adoration of the Magi, woodcut by Albrecht Dürer, Germany, 1511.)

17 The Revelation of St John came into the same tradition as the Book of Enoch. In this and other descriptions of mystical experience of the period, seven Heavenly Halls are passed through on the way up to God. The numbers, symbols and meanings echo the same laws as the pagan hierarchy, but in acceptable form, so that the gods become angels and spirits, with the uppermost expressed in seven lights. The astrological relevance of this is clear, although astrology is concerned mainly with the planetary world. (Apocalypse, engraving from J. S. and J. B. Klauber's *Historiae biblicae veteris et novi testamenti, c.* 1750.)

18 Early organized Christendom did not entirely ignore the sky; images like this planisphere survived. But there was little progress beyond the work of the Greeks. Such manuscripts, however, did preserve many ideas that might have been lost over the Dark Ages. (Ptolemaic planisphere, by Geruvigus, 9th–10th c., British Museum.)

Islam

The Arabs began with astronomy rather than astrology. They improved on instruments, and their numerals gave greater accuracy. Out of such precision came better star maps, with more detailed constellations. Later, as a consequence of the observation of celestial bodies, came an interest in astrology.

19

19 An astrologer takes a reading of the position of a star. Accuracy and authority are crucial, hence the hourglass and Ptolemy's works. The findings made by the Arabs were compiled into elaborate tables of celestial motions. (Border of miniature in Jehangis Album, Mughal India, *c.* 1618, Staatsbibliothek, Tübingen.)

20 The astrolabe was an instrument for observing and computing time, direction and position. It could be used for navigation, astronomy and astrology. The Arabs, always fine metal-workers, perfected the hand version. (Astrolabe, by Mustafa Ayyub, Islamic, 17th c., Science Museum, London.)
21 The stellar globe, which is a model of the star positions on the celestial sphere, was a vital piece of theoretical equipment to any good astrologer. There were of course many who practised

without understanding, from book learning or superstitious ignorance; but such men are found in every profession. (Celestial sphere, Islamic, *c.* 16th-17th century, Science Museum, London.)

22 The constellations of the zodiac were drawn with great care and beauty by the Arabs. However, the actual star configurations had shifted from the original positions of the zodiacal degrees plotted in pre-Greek times. This was because the signs are fixed to the position of the sun as it enters the vernal equinox; and the equinoxes 'precess' as the earth's axis tilts. So it was that astronomy and astrology began to part company, the former measured against the physical stars, the latter related to the precessional movement of the earth. (Virgo, from MS. Marsh 144, Iran, AD 1009/10, Bodleian Library, Oxford.)

20

21

23 The astrological zodiac shows the relationship of the sun to the earth, so that when the sun is in, say, Sagittarius this is a terrestrial orientation and not a stellar one. This makes the zodiac in fact part of the outer earth, as is the celestial sphere, which is only a projection of the earth's globe on to space. Astrology is the study of geocentric phenomena. (Sagittarius, from MS. of Abd al-Rahman al Sufi, Iran, 1630–31, Spencer Collection, New York Public Library.)

24 In this purely astrological view of the constellation Leo, Helios-Apollo is seen riding on the Lion's back. This is quite a different viewpoint from the astronomical in that it does not seek to match the star pattern but to express the power of the sun-ruled sign. The fiery mane of the god denotes this well. (Sun in Leo, from MS. Bodl. Or. 133, Iran, Bodleian Library, Oxford.)

25 Astrology had no small influence on Islam. Here the whirling Dervishes not only spin on the still axis of the spirit up from stones through the ladder of reality to God, but process in concert as turning planets orbiting the sun of their leader sheikh. The whole operation, or Mekabale, involves the microcosm (man) in inner and outer communion with the macrocosm. (Dervishes, from MS., Turkey, 1595, Chester Beatty Collection, Dublin.)

26 The Arab arts naturally contained astrological elements because of the Islamic fascination with the workings of fate and destiny. Kismet is a constant theme; and here, in an anthology of Persian poetry, the decorations include zodiacal signs. (Aries and Taurus, from MS. *Munis-al-Abrar*..., Iran, 1341, Metropolitan Museum of Art, New York, Harris Brisbane Dick Fund.)

27 The imagery of astrology had great appeal to the Arab heart as well as to the Arab head. In such a study poetry and mathematics blended perfectly to give insight into Heaven and Earth. (Gemini, Cancer and Leo, from MS. *Munis-al-Abrar*..., Iran, 1341, Metropolitan Museum of Art, New York, Harris Brisbane Dick Fund.)

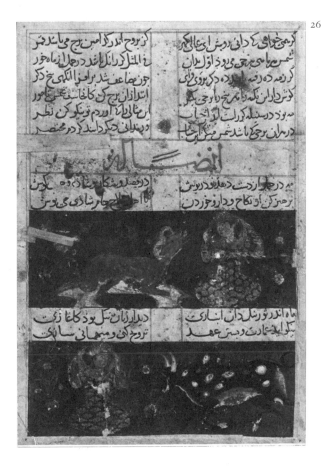

24

25

26

27

The Middle Ages

From the time of Aquinas onwards, the West took to astrology
with no difficulty. Its system fitted the philosophy and theology
accepted by schoolmen. Against the background of avid
absorption of Greek, Arab and Jewish knowledge the subject
quickly percolated throughout the intelligentsia. In time even
the universities taught astrology, although inevitably it dried
out into learned scholasticism. Much original practical work was
also done.

28 This illumination shows particular planets related to specific
great men. In this is the notion that a man has a ruling planet,
and that if he is true to it, he will live out a singular fortune.
Individual fate is only for those who live according to their true
nature. In the light of astrological theory the folk saying
'Follow your own star' takes on a real and practical significance.
(Pagan philosophers related to planets, from Codex ser. nov.
2.652, 14th c., Nationalbibliothek, Vienna.)
29 The interaction of man and heavens was studied closely,
but never to be forgotten was the fact that man as an earthbound
creature was subject to the laws of his mineral, vegetable and
animal aspects. Certainly the human soul's real home was Eden
and the spirit's abode Heaven; but man had fallen, or been sent,
into carnal existence as a husbandman, and this mundane
situation could not be ignored by astrologers. (Man and heaven,
woodcut, 16th c.)
30 The great celestial man with his body made up of the zodiac
was a synthesis of working principles, each sign depicting a
cosmic, terrestrial and organic function. Events above were
matched by response below, although not always in the most
obvious way. Thus Mars in his positive sign, Aries, might give
one man a head wound, or impel another to impulse; on a
larger scale it could initiate a daring commercial enterprise, or
precipitate war. Everyone was part of Adam, and he was a
reflection of the heavenly man. (Zodiacal man, from MS.,
Germany, 14th c., Bayerische Staatsbibliothek, Munich.)

28

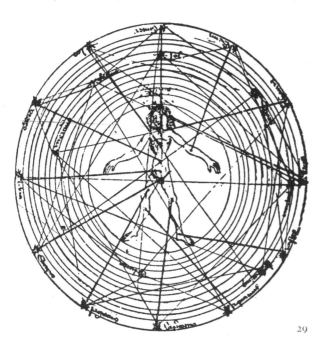

29

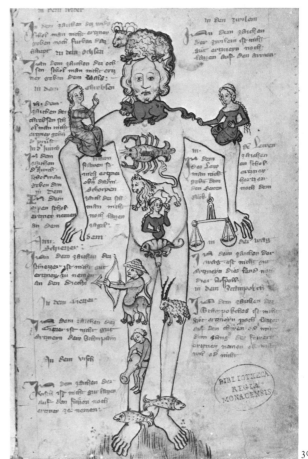

30

31

32

31,32 Instruction books have been written on astrology in every period. In this English manuscript of the thirteenth century, the children of the sun and Jupiter are illustrated. The graphic descriptions include occupations and rank, each demonstrating in the costume and custom of the age ever-recurring patterns and recognizable archetypes. (Children of the sun and of Jupiter, MS. *Boke of Astronomy*, English, late 15th c., Bodleian Library, Oxford.)

33 This page of a barber-surgeons' guildbook shows the importance of the humours and their corresponding types to a profession that adjusted the imbalance of body fluids. The treatment was usually linked with a working understanding of astrology. (Four humours, from MS. *Guildbook of the Barber-Surgeons of York*, English, 15th c., British Museum.)

33

34 The blood-letting of barber-surgeons was directly related not only to the four humours but the different zodiacal zones of the body. After astrological diagnosis the afflicted area was bled to offset the planetary pressure that affected it. (Blood-letting, woodcut, 16th c.)

35 This print by Dürer describes the symptoms of syphilis and accompanies a poem on the subject by the physician Ulsen. The disease was of plague proportions at the time and was related to a particular conjunction of Jupiter and Saturn in Scorpio. Every disease is said to have a planetary configuration, and by recognizing the pattern diagnosis is obtained. (The Syphilitic, woodcut by Albrecht Dürer, 1496.)

36 The role of astrologer became demanding enough for professionals. Many courts including that of the Pope had an astrologer. Their job was to survey the general situation and to advise on the timing of actions. The influence of the astrologer over a ruler often created jealousy amongst courtiers, and much discretion had to be exercised. (The Astrologer, woodcut, 16th c.)

37 One of the tasks of State astrologers was to forecast times of good or ill fortune for a nation. In this print Saturn in an afflicting role chastises a country. Such periods are recognizable when this planet passes through the ascendant or sun sign of a people. The year 1492 in the print was a disastrous (the word means ill-starred) one for the Jews, a people under Capricorn whose ruler is Saturn. They were deported en masse from Spain. (Saturn as ruler of the year, woodcut, c. 1500.)

38,39 The Church had employed astrological principles in its buildings since early times, although it did not recognize that the East-West axis of its sites was of much older origin than the direction of Jerusalem. By the Middle Ages there were several Church schools of astronomy, still at one with astrology. Mont Saint-Michel in France was such a place; Chartres, too, is rich in such symbolism as the sun and moon towers. In our illustrations are carvings from Amiens showing the signs and the seasonal tasks associated with them. (Zodiac signs and related occupations, relief, Amiens Cathedral, mid 13th c.)

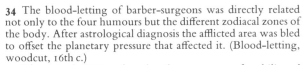

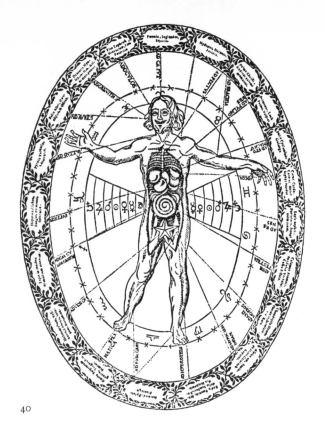

40

Renaissance

With the sophistication of the Renaissance, astrology became even more widespread. Ideas that had been confined to the world of scholars came into common use as the new rich of the commercial aristocracy established themselves as an educated class. Art and science flourished, and in the midst of creation and discovery astrology found its place in personal and public fields. Generals, architects, painters, poets, merchants and rulers used astrology in one way or another. The world was a cosmic dance, and astrology was the skill by which one might see the steps to be or not to be taken. This was the zenith of the art-science.

40 Medical astrology was developed further during the Renaissance. Here a diagram relates the organs to the planets and zodiac, matching them to animal, vegetable and mineral substances to be used in treatment. The favourable times of application are also indicated. Such a teaching aid was essential to the medical student. (Chart from Athanasius Kircher's *Oedipus Aegyptiacus*, 1653.)

41 The different carnal levels influencing a man are well illustrated in this woodcut. The mineral state was expressed in the sluggard, the vegetable in the glutton, the animal in the preoccupation with power, and vanity and the human in the development of the mind, soul and spirit. Everyone contains all these levels, and they have a bearing on how much a horoscope affects a life. None of the lower three has an individual fate. (Stages of reality, woodcut, 16th c.)

41

42   **Sonn.**

43   **Luna.**

Jupiter.   44

42–44 Here the artist sets out the occupations ruled by the sun, moon, and Jupiter. The sun is concerned with rulership and dominance, the moon with matters related to water and fecundity. Jupiter, as the planet of expansion and profound emotion, is seen manifesting through religion and magnificence. The quality of the workers subject to each god is recognized in their attitudes, status and techniques. For example the solar temperament is suited to the monarch, the saturnine (*pl. 41*) to the minister, while the jovial and martial (*pl. 40*) take care of the Lords spiritual and temporal. Mercury and Venus (*pls. 37,38*) are seen as town and country, with the moon as the principle behind the mass of people. (Sun, moon and Jupiter as patrons of certain occupations, woodcut by Hans Sebald Beham, 1530–40.)

Renaissance art

45–47 These three images are part of a 15th-century Italian series on the zodiac and gods. The first depicts the sign of Cancer and its rule over the sea and ports. The next, Luna on the chariot that bears her across the sky. The last (third from left) shows Saturn, the god of Time consuming his children. An allegorical approach is vital; nothing must be taken too literally. The inner content of a symbol must be sought like that of a parable. (Cancer, moon and Saturn, reliefs by Agostino di Duccio, Tempio Malatestiano, Rimini.)

49

47

48 Chaucer demonstrates his understanding of astrology, notably in his dissertation on the astrolabe and in the *Canterbury Tales*. The Wife of Bath, after describing her love-life with her five husbands, describes herself as 'Born under Taurus with Mars therein'. This, she declares, gives her much desire and hardihood. (Wife of Bath, miniature from MS. of Geoffrey Chaucer's *Canterbury Tales*, 15th c., Henry E. Huntington Library, San Marino.)

48

50

51

49 Botticelli, the Florentine artist, used Mars and Venus as vehicles to paint a member of a prominent city family and his mistress. He also illustrated the astrological principle of Venus's effect on the soldier god. All his defences are down, his discipline gone and his watchfulness diminished in the presence of instinctive pleasure. (Venus and Mars, painting by Sandro Botticelli, c. 1485, National Gallery, London.)

50 The zodiac in marble on the floor of the Basilica di San Miniato shows Oriental influence. Laid down in the 13th century, it reveals the Arabian source of the knowledge. (Zodiac, marble intarsia floor, San Miniato, Florence, 13th c.)
51 Dürer was commissioned to draw this zodiac in the context of the total sky. In his Germanic precision he included all the degrees and star numbers. (Celestial map by Dürer, 16th c.)

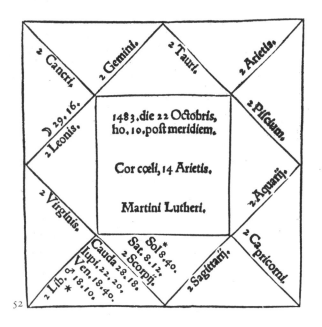

52

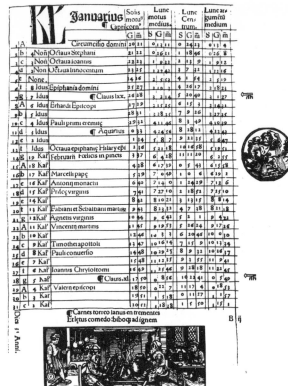

53

54

52 Martin Luther's horoscope reveals a powerful drive generated by a precise Sun and Saturn conjunction in Scorpio. Not a man of quiet diplomacy but of obsession with and against authority. (Horoscope from treatise by Jerome Cardon, Nuremberg, 1548.)

53 This page (above, right) from a calendar shows the positions of the sun and moon in the zodiac. From this, planting and sowing could be calculated, the farmer and gardener choosing the waxing or waning of the moon to accelerate or retard growth. (Page from calendar by Johannes Stöffler, 1518.)

54 The laying of a foundation stone can be timed to suit its function. The Escorial (below) has sun and moon in Aries in the tenth house, indicating enterprise and warlike achievement. The Spanish empire was governed from here. (The Escorial, engraving, Spanish, 16th c.)

55

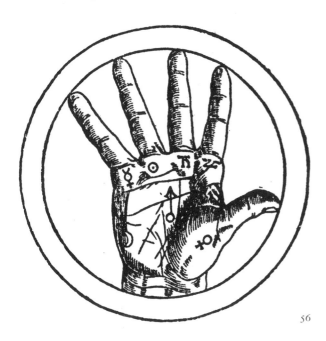

56

55 This allegory by Bovillus sets out the difference between the laws of chance and those of knowledge. On the left a blindfolded Fortuna brings men randomly into ascendancy, only to fall at the next turn, while Objective Knowledge opposite, looking into the celestial mirror surrounded by the five planets and two luminaries, sees her face and the situation clearly. (False and true wisdom, engraving, 16th c.)

56 The study of the hand and astrology have a relationship, but more by the desire of palmists than astrologers. The divisions of the zones of the hand may well embody the principles of the gods, but not in quite the same way as the planets do in a horoscope. The validity of chiromancy is not in question; but it is, like magic, another method of study. (Chiromancy, engraving, 16th c.)

57 In every age there has been popular astrology, and the Renaissance was no exception. In this page from an instruction book on the subject we see a selection of charts and commentaries. To draw up a horoscope is not beyond any intelligent person; the difficulty comes in interpretation, because of the infinite complexity and subtlety of the factors involved. One may be called a real astrologer when one no longer has to refer to books beyond those required for calculation. (Horoscopes from *Libro delle sorte*, Italian, 16th c.)

57

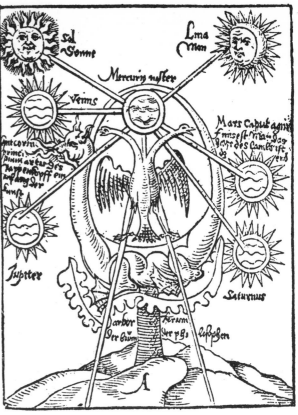

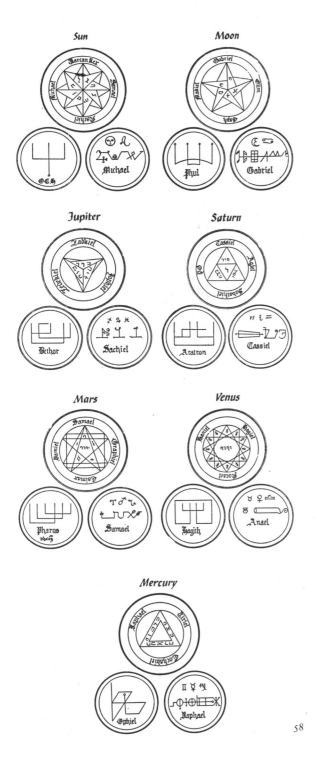

59

The Occult

Occult means 'hidden', and all the arts and sciences labelled by this name are hidden either by conscious discretion or by the very nature of their incomprehensibility to the ordinary mind. Such disciplines have always existed within human society; their function is to aid those who seek spiritual development. Their techniques and language are often obscure, in order to put off the merely curious, and to cover up operations that the orthodox would disapprove of. This practice has brought a mixed reputation. Astrology has suffered on its own account, but its involvement with other traditions has made it more vulnerable.

58 Magic borrowed greatly from astrology. Here seven pentacles, each representing a planet or luminary, blend astrology, Kabbalah, and the world of spirits or archetypes. Neither pure Kabbalah nor astrology is concerned with such evocations. (Pentacles, seals and characters of the planetary angels, redrawn from a medieval MS. *Book of Spirits*.)
59 In this alchemical diagram the planets and luminaries are clearly shown. All focus on Mercury, the mutable and transforming principle; the two-headed bird represents the active and passive principles in the alchemical operation. ('Our Mercury' as source of all transmutation, woodcut, 16th c.)

60

61

60 Astrological symbolism plays a major part in this alchemical diagram. On the holy mountain, the ancient gods, encircled by the zodiac, assist the ascent of the aspirant. The complex interaction refines the lead of base existence through the various stages of birth, death, and rebirth into the gold of immortality. (Mountain of Adepts, from Steffan Mittelspacher's *Cabala*, Augsburg, 1654.)

61 Enclosed by the four elements and the heavenly and earthly sun, moon and planets, the seven creative spirits sit beneath the active, passive and uniting principles of the trinity that governs creation. This print epitomizes not only alchemy and astrology but the teaching of all esoteric traditions. (The seven spirits which abide in the brain, from *Musaeum Hermeticum*, 17th c.)

62 This table illustrates the planetary signs corresponding to the metals, and a wide variety of alchemical signs for other substances and principles, including the four elements. The degenerate side of alchemy—those practices concerned with the purely material side of the operation—became chemistry. This science retained a residue of alchemical symbols, including the planetary ones. (Table of alchemical symbols, by John Worlidge, 16th c.)

A Table of Chymicall & Philosophicall Characters wth their significations as they are vsually found in Chymicall Authors both printed & in manuscript.

Saturne Lead		Balneü Mariæ / Balneü Vaporis / Bene / Borax		Mensis / Mercur: Jupiter / Merc: Saturn / Mer:: Sublimat
Jupiter Tinne		Cakinare / Calc / Calcviue / Calx ovorum		Nota bene / N ox: / Oleum
Mars Iron		Cayut mortis / Cæmentare / Cera / Christallum		Praecipitare / Pulvis / Pulvis Latus / Purificare / Putrificare
Sol Gould		Cinis / Cineres clavellati / Cinalar / Coagulare / Cohobatio / Crocus Martis / Crocus Veneris / Æs Viuum / Crucibulum / Cucurbitum		Quinta Essentia / Realgar / Regulus / Retorta / Sal comune / Sal Alkali / Sal Armoniac / Sal Gemma / Sal petra / Supo / Spiritus / Spiritus Vini / Strata supstrata / Solvere
Venus Copper				
Mercury Quicksilver		Dies / Digerere / Dissolvere / Distillare		
Luna Silver		Filture / Fimus Equini / Firne / Flegma / Fluere		Sublimare / Sulphur / Sulphur vive / Sulphur Philosophari / Sulphur nigru
Acetum / Acetü distillat / Æs / Ær / Alembicus / Alumen / Amalgama		Gumma		Tartar / Calx tartari / Sol tartari
Aurus / Antimonium / Aqua / Aqua Fortis / Aqua Regis / Aqua Vitæ / Arena / Arsenicum		Hora		Talcum / Terra / Tigillum / Tutia
		Ignis / Ignis rota		
		Lapis calaminaru / Lapis / Lutare / Lutum Sapientuæ		Vitriolum / Vitrum / Viride æris / Vrina
Libra / Libra semis / C	Scrupulus / Gram / Ana	Magnes / Marchsita / Materia / Matrimonii		Johannes Worlidge

62

119

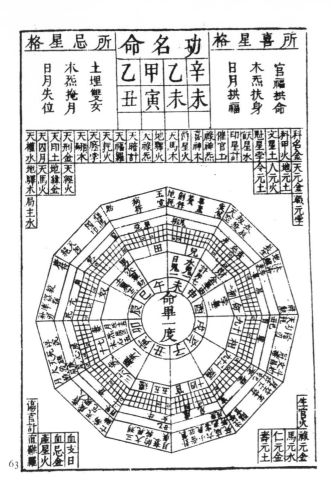

Non-Western astrology

63–65 Most highly developed societies have had astrology. In China it combines with the Taoist philosophy of twin cosmic principles, Yin and Yang. The twelve-fold division is recognizable, despite the complexity introduced by twenty-eight lunar mansions, double signs, and Yin-Yang aspects of the planets. Even among the Aztecs of Mexico, the theme of man as microcosm reappears. In India, Mesopotamian and Greek traditions have survived in Hindu guise; measurements were made in observatories like this. (Horoscope, China, 14th c.; Zodiacal man from *Codex vaticanus B*, Aztec, 15th c.; Observatory at Delhi, engraving by Thomas Daniell, 19th c.)

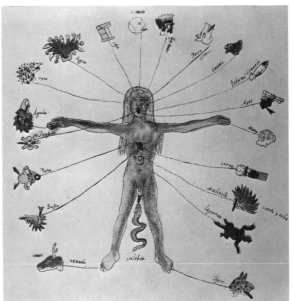

63

64

65

Transition

While the East tended to be conservative, Western astrology was changed, along with all other aspects of life, in the Renaissance. The old Julian calendar was altered to correct the year, and the new phenomenon of empirical science made inroads into classical authority. This brought about a period of transition in which the old and the new thinking blended and clashed. Astrology was caught in the middle.

66 An age which accepted the ebb and flow of celestial tides needed to know the sun sign and moon phase as well as the time of day. (Astronomical clock, Hampton Court, London, 16th c.)

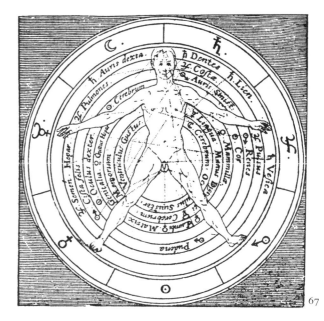
67

66

67 Even as scientists were exploring anatomy through dissection, others were still relating the sidereal (or astral) and carnal bodies. (Astral man, from Robert Fludd's *Collectio operum*, 17th c.)

68 The growth of interest in science meant that astrology was no longer taken entirely seriously. It was on the way out, along with all classical authority. (Influence of the moon on women, engraving, French, 17th c.)

68

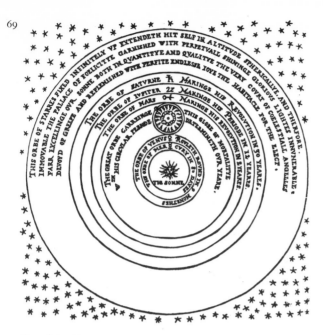

69

Coexistence

In the period which stretched from Copernicus to Newton old and new influences coexisted: revolutionary discoveries about the physical nature of the universe, alongside a continuing preoccupation with metaphysics and the spirit.

69 Copernicus' scheme, while showing the solar system in new astronomical terms, still follows the ancient view of the zone beyond the fixed stars. (Copernican world, by Thomas Digges, from Leonard Digges' *A Prognostication Everlastinge*, 1576.)

70 Galileo's telescope shattered the classical crystalline spheres. None of the planetary bodies now appeared unblemished or perfectly formed. The gods were dead. (Telescope by Galileo, 17th c., Istituto della Scienza, Florence.)

71 Through the telescope Saturn had wings, Jupiter was flattened, and Venus changed her shape. (Drawing by Galileo, 17th c.)

72 Tycho Brahe's version of the solar system retained the earth at the centre, in accordance with Scripture. (Brahe's hypothesis, from Andreas Cellarius' *Atlas coelestis*, 1660.)

73 Kepler, another astrologer-astonomer, designed his scheme of planetary relationships in Pythagorean terms: each orbit or sphere fits within a different geometrical solid. Simultaneously he was working on orbital velocities; he could accommodate both old and new views. (Harmony of the universe, from Johannes Kepler's *Mysterium cosmographicum*, 1621.)

74 Well into the seventeenth century there were still people thinking about the planets in the old way. (Title page from Michael Maier's *Viatorium*, Oppenheim, 1618.)

75,76 Robert Fludd carried on the old view. The first diagram sets up the universe in terms of musical intervals, on a great monochord stretching from heaven to earth. The second describes the relationship between macro- and microcosm. Fludd's works indicate a still considerable interest in the metaphysical outlook, although it was confined to an intelligent minority. (Title page and Music of the World, from Robert Fludd's *Utriusque cosmi . . . historia*, 1617.)

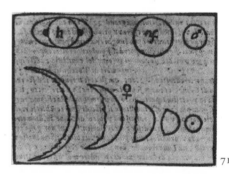

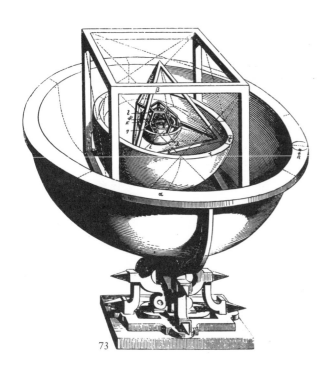

73

74

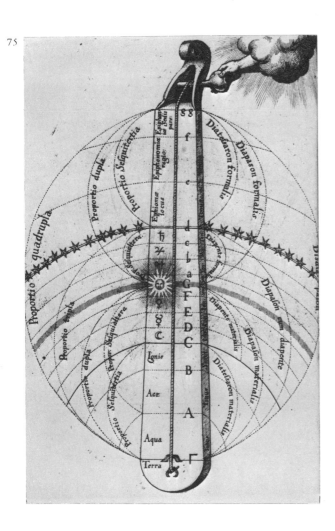

75

76

123

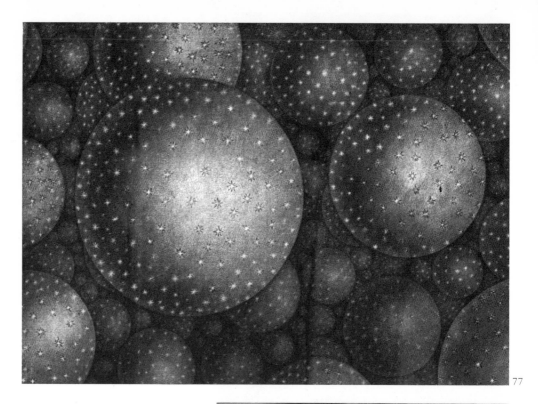

77

After Newton

At Newton's death the split between astrology and astronomy was complete. No respectable astronomer would consider astrology an exact science; and yet astrology did not die.

77 There were many new theories on the nature and origin of the universe, from Descartes' idea of huge vortices that had the celestial bodies at their focus, to the globes seen by Wright in this illustration. Most were based on gravity, rotation and spontaneous combustion. (Diagram after Thomas Wright of Durham's *Original Theory of the Universe*, 1750.)

78 With better instruments the heavens were seen as a mechanical theatre of moving bodies in various states of heat and cold. The ancient view of a living, intelligent universe had no place in the Age of Reason. (Star map from Cellarius' *Atlas coelestis*, 1660.)

79 The world beyond the planets fascinated astronomers, the Milky Way being of particular interest. Astrologers had noted individual stars, but had always taken the relative view that they were too remote to have any more than a general effect on the earth and man. (Milky Way, illustration from Thomas Wright of Durham's *Original Theory of the Universe*, 1750.)

78

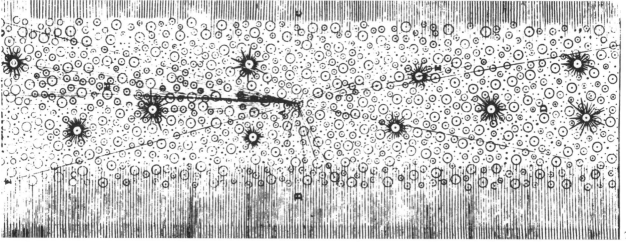

79

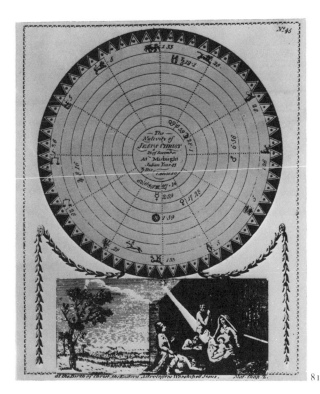

81

80

80 The practice of astrology did continue. One of its advocates was William Lilly, whose advice was ignored by Charles I to his cost. Indeed, his predictions were so accurate that when the plague and fire of London came in 1665–66 he was called before a House of Commons committee to explain his pre-knowledge. The woodcut of Gemini (the sign of London) over fire is from Lilly's forecast in 1651. (Prediction of a great fire in London, woodcut after Thomas Lilly, 1651.)

81 During this period there was a little astrological speculation. One astrologer cast Christ's horoscope, making him a Capricorn. The idea is not convincing, in that it is unlikely he was born on 25 December and because the chart is not as dramatic as might be expected. But then every field has its faulty speculations. (Horoscope of Christ, 18th c.)

82 Horoscopes of important events continued. The chart of the United States on 4 July 1776 was cast. Its character is a Cancerian family of states and communities. Moon in Aquarius gives the political ideal that all men are created equal although Mars in Gemini indicates a divided form of justice. The two benefics, Jupiter and Venus, in Cancer bode great wealth. (Horoscope of the Declaration of Independence, 1776.)

82

	SIGN	DATES	RULE	ELEMENT	HUMOUR	CROSS
1	♈ Aries	21 Mar. – 20 Apr.	♂ Mars+	△ fire	choleric	cardinal
2	♉ Taurus	21 Apr. – 21 May	♀ Venus–	▽ earth	phlegmatic	fixed
3	♊ Gemini	22 May – 21 Jun.	☿ Mercury+	△ air	sanguine	mutable
4	♋ Cancer	22 Jun. – 22 Jul.	☽ Moon	▽ water	melancholy	cardinal
5	♌ Leo	23 Jul. – 23 Aug.	☉ Sun	△ fire	choleric	fixed
6	♍ Virgo	24 Aug. – 23 Sep.	☿ Mercury–	▽ earth	phlegmatic	mutable
7	♎ Libra	24 Sep. – 23 Oct.	♀ Venus+	△ air	sanguine	cardinal
8	♏ Scorpio	24 Oct. – 22 Nov.	♂ Mars– ♇ Pluto	▽ water	melancholy	fixed
9	♐ Sagittarius	23 Nov. – 21 Dec.	♃ Jupiter+	△ fire	choleric	mutable
10	♑ Capricorn	22 Dec. – 20 Jan.	♄ Saturn–	▽ earth	phlegmatic	cardinal
11	♒ Aquarius	21 Jan. – 19 Feb.	♄ Saturn+ ♅ Uranus	△ air	sanguine	fixed
12	♓ Pisces	20 Feb. – 20 Mar.	♃ Jupiter– ♆ Neptune	▽ water	melancholy	mutable

Cosmic clock

83 This diagram designed by the author is a synthesis of astrological principles. Beginning with the rim it edges our relative view of the world with the fixed stars, one half in night, the other (above the horizon of the ascendant and descendant) in day. This is the stellar background to our existence, and represents in the inner universe the spirit. Next comes the zodiac, arranged with Aries the spring sign coinciding with the dawn of a perfect equinox day of twelve hours light and dark. The winter solstice represents the noon of the spiritual year, the sun being in man the essential point of contact. The next thin band outlines the hours of a classical day with the decans or ten-degree sections and their rulers. Inside this are the mundane houses and key words which enclose a band describing the status of the planets in each sign. The four triangles of the elements, and the three crosses, come next, with the planetary rulers in their active and passive roles; this is the level of the soul. Inside these come the luminaries and planets with their gods, metals, ages of man and psychological key words: finally the elements and the three organic kingdoms. The whole sets out the interacting sets of laws that govern our psyche. Study of its dynamics in conjunction with self-examination illuminates it as a working system and philosophy of cosmic knowledge.

84 Even the geophysicists perceive connections between earth and heaven, with every cosmic fluctuation affecting organic life. Man, the most sensitive of creatures, is subject to these subtle influences; and the first astrologers defined them in symbolic form. Today astrology is in the process of restatement. However, its ideas are still best explained in allegory, because it deals with forces far beyond the reach of electron microscope or radio telescope. Our last picture is beautiful, but illuminates only a small fraction of the principle that Venus represents in the solar system, in nature and in man. (Phases of Venus, as seen from Lowell Observatory, California.)